CHANGING LANDSCAPES
OF SOUTHERN ONTARIO

CHANGING LANDSCAPES
OF SOUTHERN ONTARIO

Virgil Martin

Major funding for the publication of this volume
was provided by the Ontario Heritage Foundation,
Ontario Ministry of Citizenship and Culture.

THE BOSTON MILLS PRESS

Canadian Cataloguing in Publication Data

Martin, Virgil Emerson, 1952-
   Changing landscapes of southern Ontario

Bibliography: p.
Includes index.
ISBN 0-919783-77-5

1. Landscape changes – Ontario. 2. Man – Influence
on nature – Ontario. 3. Photography – Ontario –
Landscapes. I. Title.

GF512.05M37 1988   917.13   C88-093934-6

Published by:
THE BOSTON MILLS PRESS
132 Main Street
Erin, Ontario N0B 1T0
Tel.: (519) 833-2407
FAX: (519) 833-2195

American Association
for State and Local History
Award of Merit

Winners of the
Heritage Canada
Communications Award

Design by Virgil Martin
Typeset by Speed River Graphics, Guelph
Printed by Ampersand Printing, Guelph

We wish to acknowledge the encouragement and financial assistance
of the Ontario Heritage Foundation, The Canada Council, the
Ontario Arts Council, and the Office of the Secretary of State.

Sweet is the lore which Nature brings;
Our meddling intellect
Mis-shapes the beauteous forms of things: —
We murder to dissect.

Enough of Science and of Art;
Close up those barren leaves;
Come forth, and bring with you a heart
That watches and receives.

> *William Wordsworth,*
> *"The Tables Turned," 1798*

All change is a miracle to contemplate; but
it is a miracle which is taking place every
instant.

> *Henry David Thoreau,*
> Walden, *1859*

Front cover: Trent Canal Lock and Dam No. 2, June 12, 1930,
(photographer unknown, PUBLIC ARCHIVES CANADA PA-43495),
and the same view on June 2, 1986, showing Highway 401.
See page 178.

Frontispiece: Blizzard in early March, 1986, near Winterbourne
(Waterloo R. M.).

Foreword

WHAT A delight to have the privilege of introducing this book to what I hope will be a wide readership. And what a day to do the writing: a sunny, hot Easter afternoon in mid-April, with a clear robin's egg blue sky overhead and the rich, full trill of the bird itself ringing frequently outside the window. Beyond the window I gaze upon downtown Waterloo, a low-slung place with four or five high rises extending eight or ten storeys above the old skyline. In the foreground and to the left, or north, are newer multi-coloured residential subdivisions, very different from the buildings of the old town. Yes, the landscape of Waterloo is changing very rapidly indeed, especially with the building boom of the past year. The changes have been extensive, too, with the subdivisions of the last decade almost certainly covering a larger area than the old town and threatening to cover a much larger one in the next ten years. Indeed, a landscape is passing before the largely unseeing eyes of the residents of the region. I know of no attempts to measure the pace and extent of these changes, although it could be done by comparing old and new air photographs, maps, and other records of landscape, past and present.

It is concern for such landscape changes and the photographs and other evidence of them that is the subject of this new book by Virgil Martin, who previously has written along similar lines The Early History of Jakobstettel, *an account of the people and the land in and around St. Jacobs, Ontario. In this new book the author covers a wider field, portraying changes in landscapes across Southern Ontario. The landscapes are chiefly rural, but also urban, from the eastern counties of the province, west through Toronto and region, to London and beyond. The story is presented vividly with the aid of old and new photographs in pairs, "before and after" pictures of the same localities. These contrasting photos often show striking changes and sometimes surprisingly small ones, even where the old photos date well back into the nineteenth century.*

Mr. Martin's writing is very clear, and often both simple and rich. Whether dealing with agriculture, hamlets, towns, industry, or future landscapes, he strikes at the essence of his concern, making landscape come alive. He provides an interesting appendix on the technical aspects of the rephotography process that made it possible to create counterparts to the many images he had found of the past. Virgil Martin is one of the relatively few persons that I know of in Canada who is an active student of landscape. It is a neglected part of our intellectual and aesthetic domain, and one that can tell us much of past technology, economy, perceptions, attitudes, values, and many other aspects of our changing humanity. His book very much deserves to be read and I am sure it will enrich the lives of you and your friends.

Gordon Nelson
Waterloo, Ontario
19 April, 1987

Dr. Nelson is currently teaching Geography, and Urban and Regional Planning at the University of Waterloo. His wide-ranging interests centre on land-use history and landscape change. A prolific writer, Dr. Nelson is a frequent contributor to books and periodicals on these and related topics.

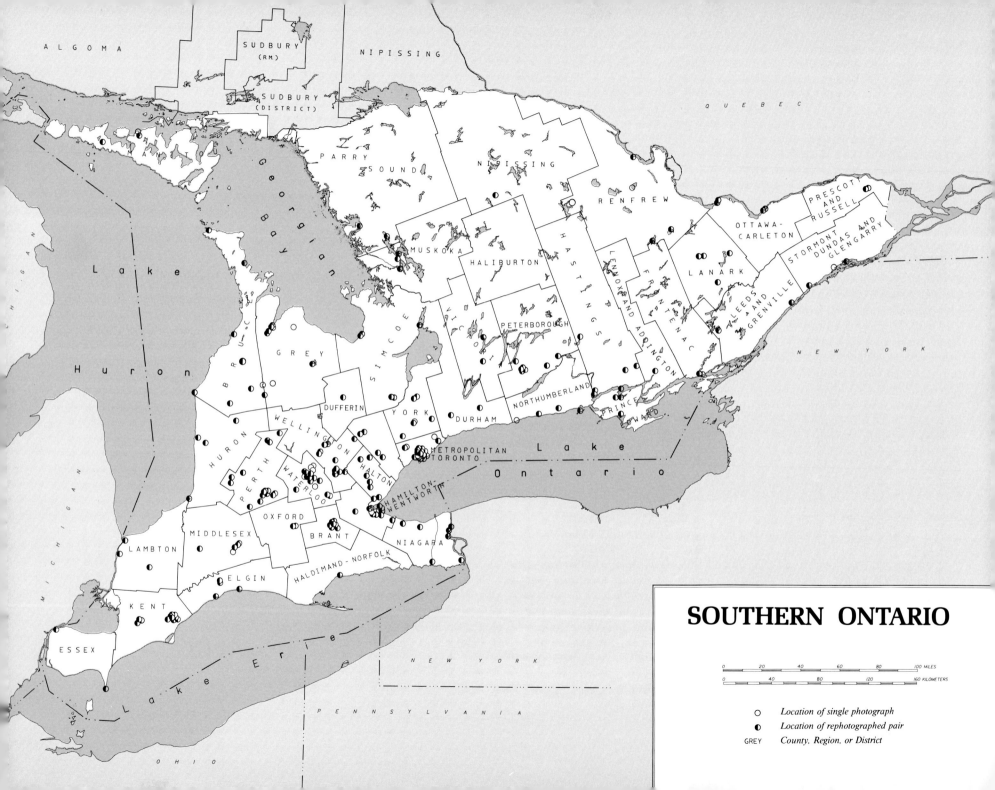

SOUTHERN ONTARIO

○ *Location of single photograph*

◑ *Location of rephotographed pair*

GREY *County, Region, or District*

0   20   40   60   80   100 MILES

0   40   80   120   160 KILOMETERS

Table of Contents

Acknowledgements

EVERY BOOK, I think, begins as one person's idea, but ends having been the effort of many. And to the many, invariably I'm sure, is owed more than a passing reference on a page that most readers skip over.

This book owes more than usual to "Anon." Nearly half of the photographs (excluding my own) were made by unknown hands, and these photos are labelled with a question mark in the credit lines. In addition, my endless searches for photos, information, and locations were greatly assisted by many people in communities across the province, from Amherstburg to Hawkesbury to Meldrum Bay—so many that to list them all would be impossible. To list those whose names spring to mind would be unfair to the anonymous majority. So to all who contributed in so many intangible ways—thank you! I hope your enjoyment of the book is an adequate remuneration.

Nearly half of the old photos were selected from the National Photography Collection, Public Archives Canada, a fact which made the friendly, professional cooperation of the Public Service Section staff pivotal to the project. Other photos came from the following collections: Brant County Museum, Brant Historical Society, Brocksden Country School Museum, Bruce County Museum, City of Toronto Archives, County of Grey Museum, Forwarders' Museum (Prescott), Gore Bay Museum, Guelph Civic Museum, Guelph Public Library, Hamilton Public Library, Hastings County Historical Society, Kent County Museum, Lambton Heritage Museum, Lennox & Addington County Museum, Meaford Museum, Middleville Museum, Ministry of Natural Resources, National Air Photo Library, Newmarket Museum, Oil Museum of Canada, Ontario Ministry of Agriculture and Food, Ontario Archives, Ontario Hydro Archives, Peterborough Centennial Museum and Archives, Point Pelee National Park, Ridgetown Historical Society, Stratford-Perth Archives, Vankleek Hill Public Library, and the Wellington County Museum and Archives. I also thank the following businesses for supplying photographs: Commonwealth Historic Resource Management Limited, Douglas Paisley Studio Ltd., James Studio, Windsor Star, Tom Bochsler Mainway Studio, and The Roy Studio. And finally, the following individuals kindly loaned photographs from private collections: Perrin Beatty, MP, the Dodds family, J. A. Morris, Allan D. MacKinnon, Bob Martin, Mary Anne Roberts, B. (Jim) Smith, and Marvin C. Smith.

During this project I lived, at various times and places, with Chris, Dale, Ken, Janet, Ken, Eugene, Sandi, Jim, Jim, and Beth, who put up with my inevitable ups and downs, and said the right things when I felt inclined to produce a good draft by stoking the wood stove with the half-finished manuscript. Beth helped with typing and with a host of details and lists. She also provided solutions to some literary conundrums, and invaluable companionship and support. Marcia and Janet helped with the final retyping of the manuscript. I am also grateful to many other friends who offered timely encouragement and suggestions, and especially to Moe and Sue, and Allen and Donna, who provided homes away from home.

André Probst skilfully piloted a plane over Hamilton Harbour so that I could rephotograph obliques in that vicinity. Lionel Monroe piloted his boat to an otherwise inaccessible point on the Ottawa River, and gave me a colourful historical tour in the bargain.

My father proofread most of the early drafts. Terri Macli edited a later version and suggested many worthwhile revisions. Paul Litt provided invaluable, constructive criticism and made many contributions to the polish of the manuscript in its final stages. Responsibility for factual accuracy remains mine, however, and corrections are welcomed.

Financial assistance to undertake the project came from the Explorations program of The Canada Council. The Ontario Arts Council, through The Boston Mills Press, contributed to the acquisition of photos. The Ontario Heritage Foundation provided financial assistance for editing and printing. Finally, Michael McDonald of Ampersand Printing and John Denison of The Boston Mills Press deserve special mention, not only for their generous cooperation and assistance, but also for letting me do it my way.

Facing page: Trout Lake, Nipissing Dist., July 24, 1983.

Introduction

THE IDEA seemed quite simple. I reasoned that by using clues in an old photograph it should be possible to locate the exact spot where the photographer had set up his tripod. Then, by carefully matching the season, time of day, and light conditions, a photograph very similar to the original could be produced. A comparison of the photos would highlight the changes that had come about during the intervening years.

Practical testing of the idea, using some old photos at hand, soon demonstrated that the basic premise was valid. It also indicated that I should expect a very broad spectrum of changes in both rural and urban settings—including changes so radical that some scenes might be impossible to match.

But most outdoor photographs can be rephotographed from precisely the same point of view, provided that the location is identified. This seems so obvious that I wondered then, and still do not know, why such before-and-after pairs are not a more prominent feature of history books. The few examples I found convinced me that such pairings conveyed far more information about a place than could single photos. Rephotography reduces ten years, or a hundred years, to a flash between two frozen moments, creating a sensation of time travel which tweaked my imagination and inspired this book.

The first part of the project, and in many ways the easiest, involved finding old photographs and selecting those which were suitable. It soon became evident that most pictures record people and events; those that explicitly depict places are far less common. On average, perhaps one percent of the photos I looked at fell into the "potentially useful" category. There was, however, no shortage of material to sift through. The huge collection of Public Archives Canada, Ottawa, provided an almost inexhaustible source, but visits to dozens of smaller archives, museums,

libraries, and private collections also produced many interesting finds. In fact, there was soon too much material for the time I had allotted to fieldwork. During several seasons of travel and photography I was frequently reminded that there must be thousands of potentially useful photos still awaiting discovery.

Finding the locations depicted by the photographs was sometimes straightforward and sometimes hopelessly difficult. Before attempting to zero in on a difficult location, some time was spent examining the photo with a magnifying glass. Topographical maps, aerial photographs, local history books, directories, and a gazetteer also furnished leads. Most challenges were resolved with the help of keenly interested individuals whose knowledge of local history and geography was invaluable.

The moment of discovery—finding a new and unfamiliar place as it is today, after having grown familiar with an old photograph—is a thrill that I will never grow tired of. I hope the photos convey some of the sheer adventure that accompanied every successful search.

In doing the fieldwork for this book, I encountered a variety of obstacles. Newly built walls were not unusual. Massive excavations or the demolition of a building sometimes left a point of view dangling high in the air and out of reach. Occasionally a road surface had been raised so that an original camera position was now "six feet under," and a few points of view were lost beneath man-made lakes. The most common obstruction, however, was trees. Left to themselves, trees will grow anywhere and everywhere; it was not unusual to find a forest scene where an old photograph clearly showed open fields.

Because of these obstacles, I often had to be satisfied with an imperfect match. Where a view was obscured, it seemed more honest and certainly more meaningful to try to capture the feeling of a place with an angle that

Facing page: Upper Canada Village, Stormont Co., July 2, 1983.

mimicked the original, rather than blindly adopting the precise point of view. When even this compromise was not practical, I shot a collection of details for the purpose of illustrating the temporal relationships of various elements in the landscape.

By far the greatest satisfaction came with the discovery of unobstructed and attainable points of view. The location of the precise camera position was found by relating the positions of objects in the fore- and middle-ground to those farther away. Buildings, particularly chimneys and roof lines, were especially useful in this regard, but many other natural and man-made features—cliffs, hills, shorelines, fences, roads, power lines—were also used in this simple version of a surveyor's resection.

Fortunately, it is not essential that views be matched exactly in order to draw useful comparisons. The critical reader will find various degrees of camera-position mismatching despite reasonable efforts to minimize such errors. In addition to the problem of obstacles mentioned above, errors occurred when there was not enough useful detail remaining of the original scene, or because I misjudged a critical angle. (It is impractical to arrange precise compositions with cars racing by on either side!) In the darkroom, I was dismayed to find that even slight differences in perspective, undetected in the viewfinder, became quite apparent when the prints were made.

Seasonal change in this part of the world is dramatic and lends character and appeal to our culture and our landscapes. However, it is not the intention of this book to look at the impact of weather and changing seasons. A deliberate attempt was made to minimize this aspect of landscape change in the paired photos. Winter scenes, relatively scarce to begin with, were shunned because it was felt that variations in snow cover would tend to obscure the more substantial changes in the environment.

Photographs illustrating cultural landscapes (as opposed to wilderness scenes) were favoured for several reasons: they were much more plentiful than those of less disturbed places, and their locations were more readily identifiable and accessible.

Landscapes, being exceptionally patient and well-lit subjects, were popular among early photographic experimenters. The oldest photograph in this book dates from 1856, so the longest interval between any of the nearly 200 paired photos is 131 years. Several photos date from the 1860s, and each decade thereafter is represented. During the "Gay Nineties," seemingly every village, town, and city in the nation was photographed by professionals. These brown-toned prints have enjoyed a good survival rate and are well represented here. Then, around the turn of the century, the folding camera and the automobile began to popularize landscape picture-taking, a trend which continued to grow until the onset of the Depression. From this point onward the photos come from increasingly diverse sources. Rapid change during recent decades is illustrated by numerous pairs separated by twenty-five years or less, and is evident even in thirteen months, the shortest interval between a pair of photos.

Chapters were developed by choosing some important themes in the landscape, and then, somewhat arbitrarily, assigning photographs to one chapter or another. No attempt was made to use the chronological order of the photos. Some subjects are grouped within chapters, however, there are few photos which could not have been used just as effectively in some other chapter. The landscape exists as a continuum; sharply defined divisions can never be entirely satisfactory.

Each chapter is introduced with a brief essay. The subjects and perspectives of these essays are intended to be as diverse and liberally interwoven as the landscape itself. Being complex mixtures of interrelated and inseparable parts, landscapes can offer an inexhaustible source of awe and wonder to those who take the time to contemplate them.

The captions accompanying the photos are intended to provide basic information as well as a few points of interest about the changes in each pair. Common sense and limited space, however, imposed constraints, and it is left to the reader to explore and interpret the bulk of the photographic evidence.

An old photograph is a fossilized window through which we can gaze into the past. Without a photograph, any attempt to reconstruct a former landscape must rely on painted pictures or written accounts, both of which are products of the memory or imagination of the fallible, subjective human mind. The invention of photography brought new objectivity to the task of creating and preserving accurate images of the world around us, though it by no means removed all subjectivity from the problem.

The realism inherent in a photographic landscape anchors the image securely in both place and time. Every photograph is like a thin slice of time, one moment in an infinite succession of moments, each made unique by relentless change. Change is the sole manifestation of the passage of time; without it we have no sense or measure of time. Rephotography enhances the contrast between then and now, and helps to bring the passage of time into sharp focus.

History, as it is commonly understood, is backward looking: its aim is to illuminate the past. But surely its greater purpose is to explain the present—to shed light on how and why the past has shaped our present world. Taking random bits of history in the form of old photographs as starting points, this book travels forward in time to discover what has become of these places. In this way, the present is treated as the future-already-here. Unlike conventional history, the observer is oriented in a forward direction—a fresh outlook which can be helpful in understanding the present or anticipating the future.

Like the six blind men of Indostan grasping to define an elephant, specialists within isolated scholarly disciplines may observe certain facts about landscapes, but they are unlikely to offer a well-rounded understanding of them. Even when the various descriptions of the elephant—snake, spear, fan, wall, tree, and rope—are combined, the essence of the beast is not revealed. And landscapes are far more variable than elephants. Perhaps this explains why so little has been written on the subject of landscape evolution—very little, considering that landscapes are everywhere around us.

What is offered here might be classified in academic terms as an informal photographic investigation of the shaping and changing of Southern Ontario's visual environment during the past 130 years. The novelty of the technique and the complexity of the subject did not lend themselves to a rigid interpretive framework. Rather, an exploratory, nonspecialist overview was adopted throughout the book—a perspective based on the notion that although landscapes are multifaceted and dynamic, they are also complete, coherent entities. Rephotography facilitates such an approach by offering pertinent information to a wide range of disciplines. And in so doing, it provides an effective medium for bridging and combining diverse areas of knowledge—which is, perhaps, a roundabout way of saying that rephotography falls within the traditions of historical geography.

Enough time has now elapsed to provide us with an opportunity to use rephotography to begin to monitor some relatively long-term changes in our environment. The paired photos are, in fact, a very-long-interval kind of time-lapse photography. When a sufficient number of locations have been rephotographed, it becomes possible to draw some general conclusions about the nature and degree of change in the landscape—conclusions which might elude a more conventional method of investigating the evolution of landscapes.

For example, the photos in this book show a rather surprising change in Southern Ontario's landscape. The past century has witnessed a widespread regeneration of trees, woodlots, and forests. The area covered by forests today is only a fraction of what it was before settlement began, but there has been a considerable amelioration of the stark landscapes that were so typical of the nineteenth century. With few exceptions, the pioneers hated trees, and they delighted in being able to see a considerable distance around. But times have changed and trees are now revered. Without photographic evidence, the extent of the reforestation would hardly be believable and its implications would be far less obvious. Southern Ontario's vistas are being narrowed and shortened, hemmed in by the regrowth of trees on every horizon, though the trend seems to have gone virtually unnoticed.

That so much once-cleared land is again overgrown with trees is a reminder that our occupation of this country is very recent, and that our understanding of its resources has been fraught with misjudgment and shortsightedness. The returning forest is a direct result of the changing economics of farming, but it also reflects a new sense of environmental stewardship. Ironically, both changes are readjustments and adaptations to the revolutionary advance of technology into all aspects of our culture and our lives.

In general, the photos also indicate a closely related but more disturbing trend that is evident in both rural and urban areas. Landscapes, wherever they are intensively managed, are drifting toward sterile homogeneity. Eclectic diversity is giving way to the efficient mediocrity of landscapes dominated by machines.

Despite our great experimental adventure with technology, the modern landscape is still influenced by the forces of Nature: the relentless succession of plant and animal life, and the wind and sun, the rain, and the waves. Together, Man and Nature are continually remaking Southern Ontario's landscapes. Neither works alone.

In general, the Southern Ontario landscape is a byproduct of our exploitation of Nature's provenance. Sometimes the results are exquisite, sometimes hideous, but most often they are quite ordinary. This should not, however, lull us into thinking that ordinary landscapes are uninteresting or unimportant. Though easily dismissed, every landscape is a living chronicle. Society continually writes history into its landscapes, leaving a record more detailed and vast than any other.

CHAPTER ONE

Foundations

IF A GLOBE were to be made 12 inches (30 cm) in diameter, with every detail of the earth's surface reproduced exactly to scale, the highest mountain in the Canadian Rockies would be represented by a bump roughly equal to the thickness of a single leaf in this book. In Southern Ontario, the most extreme relief occurs between Georgian Bay and Blue Mountain—a vertical difference of 1125 feet (343 m) over a distance of four miles (6.4 km). This would amount to about three ten-thousands of one inch (.008 mm) on our imaginary globe—an imperceptible ripple.

The earth's topography seems remarkably smooth when compared to the vast area of its surface. Everyday experience lets us take our perspective for granted, and we forget how lowly it is. And yet it is this worm's-eye outlook which provides us with most of our impressions of the planet and its landscapes.

This suggests a broad definition of landscape: an expanse of land usually seen from near the earth's surface, or a view or representation of such an expanse. The term has been part of the language and has had this meaning for centuries. In modern usage, the word is often given a metaphorical twist and is applied in innumerable ways having little to do with scenery. We now have the landscape of the mind, the cultural landscape, academic, economic, and literary landscapes, to mention but a few. There also are many popular derivatives: seascape, townscape, cityscape, farmscape, and even dreamscape. The shared element of meaning in all these terms is the suggestion of diverse, but interactive or interdependent, elements found in association. Diversity is usually apparent, but a sense of unity may require contemplation and familiarity. An ecological, or holistic approach is commonly invoked by these terms.

The concept of landscape rests on a dual foundation. One part is the physical reality of rocks, soil, water, atmosphere, and plant and animal life, including Man's engineering and architectural modifications. The other part is not concrete, but involves human perception and the myriad factors that colour it: cultural background, economic situation and outlook, education, childhood experiences, individual likes and dislikes, prejudices, and misconceptions.

The physical reality of landscapes is obvious, but the psychological aspect is highly personal, variable, and not easily defined. It is, however, a fundamental part of all landscapes, since landscapes are inseparable from our perceptions of them. (A "landscape" unseen by human eyes is not a landscape.) Let us say then, that a landscape is an outdoor environment *as we see it*. A single scene, therefore, may constitute as many landscapes as there are observers of it.

The term "landscape" is often, and incorrectly, used interchangeably with "environment." While the latter can be effectively quantified and studied objectively, the former is not so amenable to a purely scientific approach. Geographers have had little success in devising satisfactory quantitative landscape assessment techniques. Various schemes have been tried, but invariably, they seem to have a strong resemblance to paint-by-number kits: subtlety is sacrificed to a system of numerical abstraction. Such efforts ignore a basic fact: landscapes include an important but variable psychological component and therefore do not lend themselves to being satisfactorily quantified.

Unlike computers, humans have aesthetic sensitivity to landscapes. We have likes and dislikes, and we certainly have a persistent and often intense relationship with landscapes, though by no means always a rational or a fully conscious one.

In this chapter the photographs were selected to focus on some of the prominent and typical physical features of Southern Ontario. Various

Facing page: Janet Head, Manitoulin Island, July 6, 1983.

landforms and natural boundaries are depicted. But in every pair of photos there is also a subplot of human adaptation to, and exploitation of, the landscape. And therefore this chapter, like all the rest, is also about perceptions and attitudes, and how they have changed.

Southern Ontario is comparable in size to England or Greece, and yet it makes up only one-eighth of the province's landmass and a mere one-eightieth of Canada's total area. This is the southernmost extremity of a vast and beautiful but inhospitable country, a garden on the edge of the wilderness. It is the agricultural and industrial heartland of Canada, and home to nearly one-third of all Canadians.

Southern Ontario's major axis stretches southwest to northeast across some 500 miles (800 km). The extreme southwest corner reaches the sunny latitudes of southern France and northern California. In the north the region merges into the boreal forests of the Laurentian Shield. And yet the most northerly picture in this book was taken more than 200 miles (320 km) south of the 49th parallel!

The land is varied but without strong contrasts. There are extensive areas of gently rolling hills as well as areas that are remarkably flat. The Niagara Escarpment, which extends around the western end of Lake Ontario northward to Georgian Bay and Manitoulin Island, provides the only sharp relief. In a few places these cliffs rise 300 feet (100 m), but their average height is considerably less.

Southern Ontario is virtually an island. Its boundaries are the shores of some of the world's greatest lakes and rivers—natural facts, not artificial lines drawn across a map. And though the degree of isolation provided by these bodies of water is not great, it has been sufficient to protect a way of life and a political system that is distinctly, if only slightly, different from that of the surrounding United States.

Our first line of defence against the giant to the south—the Great Lakes and their connecting rivers—has also served as our primary line of communication. Long before the first Europeans came exploring this region, the Huron Nation and the Iroquois Confederacy to the south were using these waterways to carry on a remarkably extensive trade. Then for two hundred years the fur trade made use of the Great Lakes, especially the river route along the northern edge of our region. When pioneers began clearing farms, the pattern of settlement was primarily determined by major lakes and rivers which provided the only easy access to the new lands. These were our first highways, and to this day the Great Lakes System continues to be one of the world's busiest inland waterways.

As the tide of settlement swept inland, knowledge about the suitability of various districts for agriculture began to accumulate, but not without much hardship and wasted effort. The agricultural potential of township after township was determined by a process of trial and error. A detailed picture did not fully emerge until the end of the pioneer era. Generally, the southwest and south-central regions were found to make excellent farmland, and as a result a fairly dense network of towns and cities has grown up there. But the north and east of Southern Ontario offered mostly marginal farmland scattered in pockets between rocks and lakes. Abandonment and depopulation have followed in the wake of nineteenth-century settlement. Wishful thinking and dogged determination, colonization roads and grandiose settlement schemes could not change the physical realities of the Precambrian rocks. Rather, perceptions had to change.

In many respects, the margin of the Precambrian Shield defines the northern limit of Southern Ontario. But because this natural boundary was flouted in the mad rush to settle every possible acre, and because the hills and lakes of the Shield have become a backyard playground for the urbanized south, it deserves inclusion in our survey of landscape change. The Shield region was to have been proportionately represented in this book, but a general shortage of photographic resources and the difficulty of identifying and reaching specific localities has meant that relatively few photos were included. The Shield margin has delimited this project, just as it has so many human endeavours.

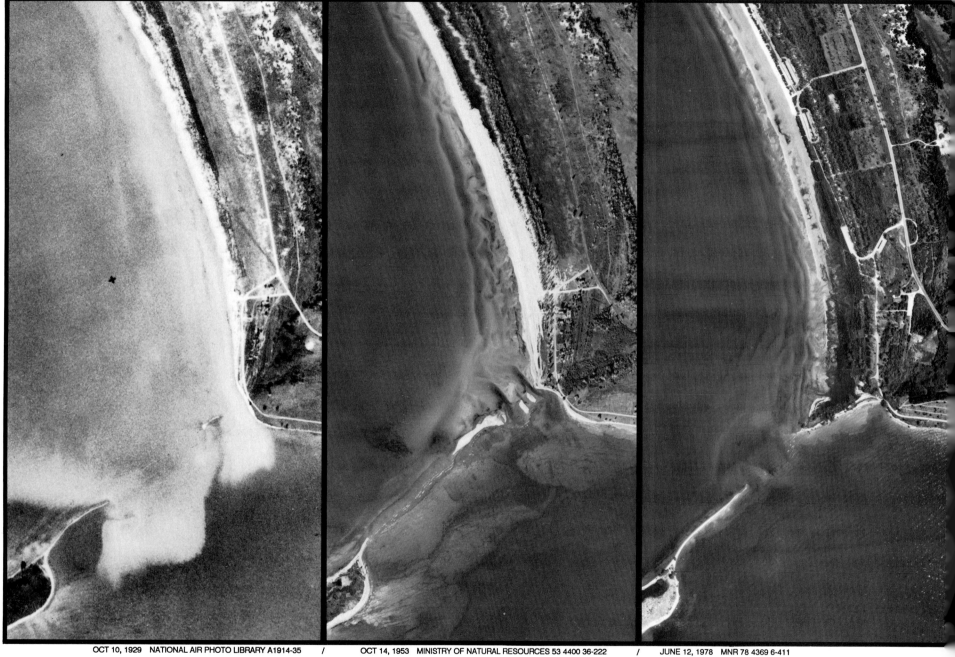

OCT 10, 1929   NATIONAL AIR PHOTO LIBRARY A1914-35   /   OCT 14, 1953   MINISTRY OF NATURAL RESOURCES 53 4400 36-222   /   JUNE 12, 1978   MNR 78 4369 6-411

NOTMAN   CA 1870   PUBLIC ARCHIVES CANADA PA-24894   /   AUG 27, 1983

17. The natural ebb and flow of Lake Ontario through the shallow straits between Owen Point and Gull Island (Presqu'ile Provincial Park) deposits, erodes, and redeposits sand, gravel, and debris. Will the ever-changing bar one day become a permanent peninsula?

18. The Niagara River has eroded a seven mile (11 km) gorge into the Niagara Escarpment. This view shows the Whirlpool Rapids where the Spanish Aereocar makes its crossing. On the right is New York State; downstream, the Niagara Glen projects from the Ontario side. Erosion has increased with the removal of trees and the trample of feet.

19. The Niagara Escarpment bisects Southern Ontario between Hamilton and Owen Sound. It provides some of the province's finest scenery and a few unusual economic opportunities as well. Lime kilns once operated along the base of the escarpment within the current boundaries of the Kelso Conservation Area (Halton R. M.). Readily accessible limestone was skidded down to the kilns for processing. On the right, the cliff face has been reworked by quarrying.

19

W. J. TOPLEY CA 1911   PAC PA-9774

AUG 20, 1983

20. The escarpment has a considerable impact on agriculture—both positive and negative. On the Niagara Peninsula it provides shelter and enhances the ameliorating effect of Lake Ontario on the local climate. Tender fruits have been grown in abundance here since the early years of settlement.

Forest regrowth along many sections of the escarpment is closing off the view of the vineyards and orchards below. This view looks out over an area near Winona and the E. D. Smith processing plant, but it had to be mismatched by a quarter mile (.5 km) to catch a last glimpse behind the green curtain.

21. Some parts of the escarpment lie buried under glacial till, but the rugged topography generally makes these areas unsuitable for farming. This section near Acton (Halton R. M.) is now rapidly reverting to forest. An elevated perspective was used to see out over the trees.

1955 (?) / SEPT 23, 1983

22. The cliffs and steep hills of the Niagara Escarpment are exceptional features of the Southern Ontario landscape; more typical are the acres of gently rolling or nearly flat cropland, dotted with a regular pattern of farmsteads and neat woodlots. This view in Hibbert Township (Perth Co.) undoubtedly has a counterpart in any of the more than 200 townships where farms *are* the landscape. And yet there are characteristic details in this scene—the long lanes and the lay of the land; the size, style, and condition of houses and barns, and the landscaping of their yards; the fences, trees, and crops—which suggest that this place is in the southern part of the Canada Company Tract.

23. From gravel to boulders, rocks are a common hindrance to farming, particularly in Eastern Ontario. Borrowman's Rock, near Middleville, (Lanark Co.) is a well-known local landmark, dumped here by the retreating ice of the last continental glacier. At one time, plans were made to get rid of this boulder and blasting holes were drilled in it, but the job was never finished and today it remains as a part of a fence and the landscape. The fragile glass-plate negative was broken at some time before the print was made.

23

By 1900, the demand for new farmland had pushed the agricultural frontier northward onto the Precambrian Shield where timber resources were rapidly dwindling. But the poor, thin soils were unsuitable for farming; they produced only hardship and broken dreams. Then, just as the harsh reality of the Shield country was settling in, a new opportunity developed as summer vacationers looked north for an escape from the city.

24. This small farm on the shore of Butterfly Lake, Muskoka District, was on the main road in 1919. However, there was no real hazard to the family cow because cars were scarce and slow. Today, a highway on the far side of the lake bypasses this place. Forest regrowth made it necessary to bring the camera approximately to the position of the car in the older picture in order to photograph recognizable landmarks.

25. Tourism was already of some importance when, in 1907, the railway reached Bala, making it the most accessible point on the Muskoka Lakes. During the heyday of travel by rail and steamer, three trains arrived here daily. The dam in the foreground replaced an older structure behind the camera.

25

PAC PA-67284   CA 1904   /   F. W. MICKLETHWAITE

PAC PA-67336   CA 1907   /   F. W. MICKLETHWAITE

JULY 21, 1983   /

JULY 21, 1983   /

Hidden away in the labyrinth of the Muskoka Lakes, dozens of hotels and lodges catered to summer fun seekers. Guest lists included names such as Carole Lombard and Clark Gable. The eventual demise of these retreats was closely linked with the displacement of trains by automobiles, of steamers by outboards, and the lodges themselves by private cottages. These changes are reflected in the landscape.

26ab. At Port Sandfield, a narrow channel connects two of the larger lakes. As late as 1950, three steamers might pass this point in a single day; but now only one remains to make a nostalgic run once or twice each summer.

26cd. As a trans-shipment point for the Parry Sound area, Port Cockburn was a fairly prosperous village. Improvements to road and rail networks, reduced lumbering activity, and fires, including one that destroyed Summit House, were responsible for the village's decline. A private residence and a little chapel are all that remain.

27. Just west of Parry Sound, the Rose Point Hotel grounds included an extensive vegetable garden, a water tower, and numerous outbuildings. Today the Rose Point Marina operates from this site. The view of it is slightly to the left of the original.

28.   An abundance of natural harbours around the eastern end of Lake Ontario meant that only those which were best situated and favoured by chance were likely to develop. At first glance, the inlet below the hamlet of Crofton (Prince Edward Co.) would appear to offer a natural harbour, but the water is very shallow far out into the bay.

The moderating effect of Lake Ontario makes this one of the best apple growing regions in the country. A few trees of the orchard in the 1913 photograph remain today, neglected, but still producing apples.

29.   In 1673, Count Frontenac, Governor of New France, travelled up the St. Lawrence by canoe. At that time, the colony had no military outposts beyond Montreal, and upon reaching Lake Ontario, Frontenac determined that a fort at the mouth of the Cataraqui River would serve to protect the fur trade. Kingston has remained an important military centre to this day. This view is to the west from Fort Henry (built in the 1830s) looking across Navy Bay to the Royal Military College, with Kingston Harbour and the "Limestone City" in the background.

OCT 1, 1983   /   W. J. TOPLEY   1913   PAC PA-10567

J. BOYD   AUG 15, 1925   PAC PA-87158   /   JUNE 19, 1983

(?)   CA 1923   PAC PA-31225   /   AUG 30, 1983

J. BOYD   SEPT 23, 1915

AUG 28, 1983   /

30ab. The sheltered fjord of Owen Sound is one of the best of many good natural harbours on the upper Great Lakes. At the mouth of the Sydenham River, which forms the inner harbour, there have been many changes since 1925—the moorings, hydro poles, lights standards, trees, and all the buildings—virtually everything is new and different, yet the overall impression is one of remarkably little change.

30cd. In contrast, things have changed dramatically at Port Stanley on Lake Erie. Through extensive dredging and filling, and the building of a breakwater, an unsatisfactory natural harbour has been greatly improved. Having no competitors, Port Stanley has become a busy facility serving the inland cities of St. Thomas and London.

The bluffs in the background are typical of Erie's north shore. Wave action and slumping soil can move the shoreline inland at an alarming rate, but here the new harbour appears to have brought erosion to a standstill.

31. Picturesque Port Dover, in the lee of Lake Erie's Long Point, has been and still is mainly geared to the fishing industry. You can smell it in the air, and hear it in the talk on Main Street and in the excited cries of gulls overhead.

ONTARIO MINISTRY OF AGRICULTURE AND FOOD 11A-58-65   (JUNE 1958?)   (?)   /   JULY 4, 1984

32. The village of Tobermory, strategically located on the northern tip of the Bruce Peninsula, is the mainland departure point for the Manitoulin Island ferry. In recent decades, the harbour has undergone extensive changes to accommodate a new ferry (its raised prow is visible beyond the motel) and a rapidly expanding tourist trade. Scuba diving is just one of many attractions; divers can explore scores of shipwrecks that resulted from tragic encounters with the area's violent storms and incredibly jagged shoreline. The area off shore was initially protected as Fathom Five Provincial Park, and has recently become Canada's first national marine park.

33. The lighthouse at Point Clark on Lake Huron was built in 1859 to warn mariners of a dangerous shoal two miles (3 km) offshore. The tower's massive limestone walls, five feet (1.5 m) thick at the base, taper upward to a height of eighty feet (24 m). While no longer necessary for safe navigation, the lighthouse is preserved as a National Historic Site. There has been some encroachment by cottages, making duplication of the precise point of view impossible, but the structure is still a photographer's delight from any angle.

34. Although mining has not figured prominently in the development of Southern Ontario, occasionally— particularly in Eastern Ontario—it has spurred the growth of a settlement, such as this one at Black Donald (Renfrew Co.). High quality graphite was discovered here in 1889. Mine shafts eventually followed the black vein under Whitefish Lake and several times the mine was flooded, only to be re-opened. But in 1954, all mining ceased and the residents gradually drifted away. In 1967, what little remained of the town site was flooded by Centennial Lake for a hydro-electric power development at nearby Mountain Chute.

35. This view of the Elora Gorge dates from 1856, only thirty years after land clearing had begun in this vicinity. As was the case throughout Upper Canada, the natural vegetation was almost entirely removed. Only on the cliffs did the cedars escape the combined onslaught of axe and grazing cattle. By making the gorge visible and accessible, the pioneers no doubt felt that they were enhancing the beauty of this natural wonder. Could they see it today, they would probably be amazed and disappointed by the regrowth of the trees.

CHAPTER TWO

Agriculture

THE HISTORY of agriculture in Southern Ontario is a large part of the history of the province, and it forms an even larger part of the history of Southern Ontario's landscapes, for the business of farming is the business of modifying the landscape to suit human ends.

Long before the arrival of European farmers, there were already a few cultivated clearings. Corn, squash, beans, and tobacco grew among charred or girdled tree trunks in small, scattered patches. The Natives of Southern Ontario were developing an agricultural way of life as their crops became adapted to this climate. There was, however, only a limited and temporary impact on the landscape as the depleted and weedy plots were left to Nature after about a decade of cultivation.

The beginning of modern agriculture in Southern Ontario is marked by the use of metal implements and, more importantly, by the introduction of animal husbandry. Cattle, horses, sheep, pigs, chickens, and bees were all introduced to this country by Europeans. With this entourage of foreign animals, the pioneers' impact on the landscape was far greater than that of aboriginal agriculture.

Oxen and horses not only made possible the clearing and cultivation of vast acreages, but the animals themselves made relatively large farms essential. Livestock also required fences, and fences depended on fixed property lines and long-term occupation of the land. Barns were built primarily for animals and their fodder. Roads, too, would have served no purpose without beasts of burden. In short, the pioneer's way of life was structured by husbandry, and it followed that the appearance of the landscape was largely determined by this symbiosis between humans and domestic animals.

Sedentary agriculture brought a completely new landscape to the seemingly endless forest. Charred stumps mingled with foreign weeds; crude fences defended the new clearings against livestock that roamed freely for most of the year; muddy, often impassable roads barely connected new farmsteads which consisted of little more than a few small log buildings set against the stark, gaping forest edge. Such were the common elements of the frontier scene.

The frontier was brutal, revolutionary, and chaotic, but it was short-lived. The forests were chopped and burned, often at an annual rate of several acres for every man in a newly opened township. This created a fast-moving front which, in a few generations, had removed most of the trees from Upper Canada's good agricultural land and also from some land that would have been better left in forest.

The philosophy of progress, and the concepts of land ownership and the freeholders' rights to use and abuse their land for personal gain were well developed and unchallenged tenets of European culture, but only in the New World could these transplanted ideas grow without constraints. The settlers' guidebooks never tired of pointing out that the land in Upper Canada could readily be made to yield a bountiful surplus; a litany of success stories proved the point. But in those early days there was very little concern for wasted timber, declining wildlife, lowered water tables, or the rapid depletion of soils. The outlines of rural Ontario's landscape emerged in an atmosphere of shameless opportunism.

Hard on the heels of the wood-chopping pioneer came the wheat farmer. Newly cleared fields, rich in nutrients, produced amazing yields of wheat, a crop which could be stored and transported readily. Other crops were grown as well, but they were mostly for consumption on the farm. Wheat supplied the revenue which allowed the first generation of farmers to make improvements to their holdings.

Fields were enlarged and cleared of stumps and rocks, and ditches were

Facing page: Bighead Valley, Grey Co., June 20, 1983.

dug. Mile upon mile of fencing was built—some of stone and some of pine stumps, but by far the most common was the zig-zag cedar rail fence. Substantial houses of squared logs or frame construction were built to accommodate large and growing families. The old log cabin then became a cow shed or hen house. New barns were also built. But farmsteads retained a rather bleak appearance, with few shrubs or shade trees and little paint to brighten the scene.

Wheat farming had some serious drawbacks. On light soils in particular, yields began to decline sharply after a few years. Weeds and wheat rust, a fungus disease, became widespread, and to compound these difficulties, prices fluctuated widely. Crop rotation was introduced to alleviate some of these problems. By including legumes in the rotation, soils were replenished and cattle better fed. But perhaps the biggest advantage of crop rotation was that, with the help of improving local markets, it diversified the farm economy. The mixed-dairy farm was born.

Diversity also became evident in the landscape: a great variety of field crops was interspersed with pastures, woodlots, orchards, and yards which sported an amazing array of large and small buildings as well as fruit trees, lawns and flowers.

Mixed-dairy farming gave every family member, including children and grandparents, an integral role in the farm's operation. Combined with the fact that this farming strategy has been successfully pursued for more than a century, this makes it easy to understand why an idealization of farm life still has great currency, particularly among urbanites with rural roots.

But time does not stand still on the farm. Constant change and adaptation have been the lot of the Ontario farmer. Undoubtedly, the most important source of change has been the endless introduction of new machinery. By 1850, a variety of labour-saving inventions had clattered onto the scene. The rickety horse-drawn reaper, for example, could accomplish as much as nine men wielding scythes. Fewer hands in the fields marked the beginnings of a hundred-year trend toward the depopulation of rural Ontario.

There was, however, a more immediate impact on the landscape: the new machinery worked best in fields that were larger, more level, and more uniform in shape. Stones, stumps, and awkward corners exacted a greater penalty than in former times. Less desirable fields were relegated to permanent pasture—at least as long as mixed-dairy farming swayed land use decisions.

In recent years there has been a dramatic increase in the sophistication of tractors, implements, and automated farming systems. The trend is closely associated with cash cropping and specialization. Large amounts of capital are essential and large acreages are common. The effect is felt on all Ontario farms, including those which are too small to participate, but the direct impact on the landscape is most visible near cities and on the expanses of flat land in the southwest.

High-tech specialization is putting great pressure on mixed-dairy farming. By increasing the volume of production, small per-unit profit margins can be more readily tolerated by modern, big-time farmers, but the small producers feel the squeeze. For example, a neighbour's ten or twenty thousand laying hens, automatically fed and watered, make the old hen house, with its small flock of multi-purpose birds, hopelessly obsolete, if not yet extinct.

Mechanization is radically changing life on the farm. The modern farmer is a technician and a businessman, and there is less need for the active participation of the whole family. The landscape, too, is simplified and standardized in order to adapt it to the needs of machines instead of animals. Many fences have become useless in the new landscape, and they are abandoned, or removed to enlarge fields. Less visible and less permanent electric fences are strung as needed. Many pastures and odd corners are no longer grazed and now grow wild.

Some traditional two-storey barns are re-equipped with new and specialized stabling, while others fall into disuse. Long, low, metal-clad pole barns, large storage bins, and tall silos are typical of the new farm. Barns usually house just one kind of animal, and just one age group, in a controlled environment.

Farm houses have made a parallel transition by being modernized almost beyond recognition. Their yards are no longer protected by fences; at least part of the garden has become lawn; aging orchards are neglected or burned; shade trees mature and are sometimes replaced by a row of saplings.

In the foreseeable future, it seems inevitable that variety in the landscape will continue to be sacrificed in the drive toward ever greater efficiency and productivity. But surely, in the long term, variety or diversity is a better measure of the health and vigour of the land.

39. Sheep grazing contentedly on verdant pastures wrapped in transparent mists: a pastoral scene not far removed from the ideal tranquility of Eden. This is the stuff of poets' dreams. In early June of 1919, with the horrors of the Great War still echoing through his mind, the photographer must have found this place especially appealing. And perhaps he understood that he was capturing something from a former time, that the twentieth century would not have the patience to maintain this bucolic landscape.

The changes came gradually. Jobs in town meant less time for the farm; keeping sheep became a bother. Then at some point, a little nursery was begun in what had been the front pasture, but not all the trees were sold. The barn got a new roof, but lost its ventilators and its livestock; it is now used for storage. A pond was dug some years ago, but the landscaping remains unfinished. Encroaching on the scene, the roadway is in the process of being rebuilt. Only the backdrop of Rattlesnake Point (Halton R.M.) seems to be immune to the restlessness of this century.

40. Cattle grazed on an island in a sluggish meander of the Carp River, with the village of Fitzroy Harbour (Ottawa-Carleton R.M.) in the background. Intensive grazing effectively prevented the regrowth of trees, but left alone, a veritable jungle has transformed the former pasture. Elm trees still dominate the scene. However, Dutch elm disease is rapidly bringing about yet another dramatic change in this landscape.

41. Looking west from the little village of Bond Head (York R.M.), a scene from more that 120 years ago is immediately recognizable. The landforms and the road, the fields and fences, and even the buildings present a pattern that hasn't changed. But the trees have changed conspicuously. The 1860 photo shows a raw landscape recently cut out of the forest; the trees that grow here today are adapted to the new ecological circumstances, giving the landscape a mellowed look. Pines and cedars have been replaced by maples and willows.

PAC PA-9779   CA 1911   /   W. J. TOPLEY

JULY 27, 1983   /

SEPT 12, 1984 / (?) 1877 ILLUSTRATED HISTORICAL ATLAS OF THE COUNTY OF ONTARIO (BEERS & CO.), FROM A MIKA FACSIMILE

42. This 1877 illustration is typical of sketches done in the field for the many directories published during the late 1800s. It is not a photograph, of course, but despite the deliberate romanticizing of the scene, the accuracy of the architectural detail is quite remarkable. In this instance, the details are verifiable because so little has changed, although a railway cut through the farm early in this century. A caption below the drawing reads: "WoodHall: Res. of Alexander Waddel: Con.9, Lot 11, Pickering Tp., Ont."

43. The mature maples have witnessed a thorough remaking of this Logan Twp. (Perth Co.) homestead. Gone are the lilacs and old apple tree, the arbour and verandah, the ridge of grass in the lane, and the lathe-turned fence posts—all replaced by the neat, clipped lines of the 1980s. Such extensive changes in the landscaping of a yard typically indicate that there has also been a change of proprietorship.

44-5. A research farm at Arkell (Wellington Co.) represents a state-of-the-art landscape, a product of changing farm technology. In 1937, a few rock piles and large boulders were still to be found in the many rail-fenced fields, which grew a variety of crops. Today, one word describes the scene: corn.

ONTARIO MINISTRY OF AGRICULTURE AND FOOD 11A-8-000   -001

AUG 18, 1937

JULY 12, 1983   /   (?)

46. Economy of scale has enticed the family farm toward greater specialization, but high-tech farming requires large capital investments. With limited resources, farms tend to remain somewhat diversified, occasionally shifting their main emphasis of production to keep up with changing markets.

A few miles from Owen Sound, a typical family farm shows signs of having switched from dairy to beef during the twenty-one years that separate the photos. The small, cement-block milk house appears to be no longer used, and the recent addition to the barn—with large, ground-level doors permitting front-end loader access—is clearly intended for beef cattle. Note, however, that Herefords were also pasturing in the 1962 photograph.

47. In the same neighborhood, a once viable farm has gone out of business. The pictures tell the story: the barn was getting run down and obsolete; the hills behind the barn were not particularly valuable as farmland, but when the gravel in them attracted a pit operator, a comfortable retirement was ensured. The barn was razed, and a new laneway built to haul machinery in and gravel out. Only the house remains, and probably its future also depends on the demand for the gravel under it.

OMAF 11A-72-50   OCT 1, 1962   /   (?)   JUNE 21, 1983

SEPT 1, 1983 / (?) SEPT 30, 1960 OMAF 11A-69-50 / ND DODDS FAMILY

SEPT 1, 1983 / (?) SEPT 30, 1960 OMAF 11A-69-51

48. Near Iona Station (Elgin Co.), we see further evidence of the trend toward specialized farming. In 1960, there were numerous small, fenced fields; sheep, chickens, and hogs can be seen in the photo. Today, the land is rented by a neighbour and it grows a single, uninterrupted cash crop: soybeans. The barn and all the activity associated with it are gone, replaced by an office for a family real estate business.

The close-ups of the house show only minor changes of detail, but the yard has been transformed by trees that were planted shortly before the oldest picture was taken. In the 1960 (middle) photo these trees have reached their prime, and newly planted shrubs appear along the foundation.

49. A long succession of generations has made a living from the shallow soils of this Belleville area farm. The remarkable stability of the landscape is maintained by an enduring family structure that clearly makes the farm its unifying theme. The house, with its dark, Victorian trim and cedar shakes, attracts the attention of tourists who happen this way. Beside the barn, there once were two wooden silos, but such structures have a limited life span. In the foreground, pasture has replaced buckwheat—a crop well suited to drought-prone soil, but seldom grown today.

49

50. River Lodge Farm, near Teeswater (Bruce Co.), has undergone extensive changes since 1965, including a change of ownership. A sizable addition to the barn was followed by new paint for the whole structure. But the most conspicuous and expensive addition is the silo. Most Ontario farms have added one or more silos in recent decades. The landscape is affected in two ways: first, there is the visual impact of the silo's considerable height, which changes the skyline and tends to diminish the stature of adjacent buildings. Secondly, cropping practices change—more corn is grown, and fields are often consolidated.

51. Progress has put a silo here, but it has spared the carefully crafted rooftop ventilator. Like most of the small, hip-roofed barns that are so typical of Prince Edward County, this one, near Wellington, is well maintained. These barns are perhaps the single most important element in this cultural landscape in terms of imparting distinctiveness and identity. Meanwhile, the farm across the road has disappeared. Like many family farms, it was too small to be viable in today's agricultural economy; the land now enlarges the operation of another area farmer.

SEPT 25, 1983 / (?) JUNE 1965 OMAF 11A-103

SEPT 28, 1983   /   (?)   AUG 1925   PAC PA-26928

SEPT 30, 1983   /   (?)   AUG 1925   PAC PA-26933

52

Canada has no great ruins such as the pyramids or castles of some parts of the world. Our monuments are very recent, as is all our visible history. As though to rectify this deficiency, substantial stone farmhouses were built by the second-generation pioneers. Built to last "forever," they were an architectural expression of a manifest destiny.

52ab. Although the interior has been totally modernized and the exterior sadly defaced, this old farmhouse near Markham (York R.M.) still retains its basic form which identifies the Pennsylvania-German origins of its builders and its design. It probably dates from the 1840s.

52cd. In Smith Township (Peterborough Co.), this slightly smaller stone house was built in 1863. The ornate porch, added later, was probably not part of the original design. The view shows the gable end facing away from the road.

53. Near Palmerston, in the north of Perth County, a graceful Scottish cottage appears to be in good repair, circa 1955. No doubt, its small size brought about its replacement. Will the thoroughly modernized scene (shown in a wider view) survive for a century? Or even for a generation? The rail fence around the yard, a rehabilitated relic, ironically suggests that our visible past is destined to remain short-lived.

CHAPTER THREE

Urban Frontier

SURROUNDING EVERY city and most towns and villages in Southern Ontario there is a frontier—an area where farmland is being transformed into city. From our car windows, this transformation appears to happen quite suddenly. But if we stop to look around, we can see both subtle and dramatic changes in the rural landscape occurring years in advance of urbanization. Usually there is a lull of twenty or thirty years or more between the first round of speculative real estate purchases and the beginning of major construction projects. In the meantime, a unique landscape exists—a temporary landscape in transition between two relatively stable but totally different states. It is a varied landscape, though not an especially pretty one. Everywhere on the frontier there is a disquieting air of impermanence.

As urban expansion progresses on this frontier, it snuffs out the life of the very farms which once nurtured and fed the city that now looms on the horizon. For farms on the city's outskirts, it is just a matter of time until all that *has been* will be erased and forgotten and an entirely new order in the landscape will be created.

It is no mere coincidence that our fastest growing towns and cities are situated in the midst of some of the best agricultural land in the country. Historically, farm incomes provided the economic base for urban development in Southern Ontario. Furthermore, modern land developers value the same qualities that characterize superior farmland—moderate climate, good drainage, and relatively little slope. Little wonder then that our cities have acquired the nasty habit of biting the land that feeds them.

An urban frontier exists only where there is an expectation of urban growth. Speculation can drive the price of farmland up to levels where it no longer makes sense for a farmer to continue his operation, no matter how productive. Though often referred to as development "pressure,"

high prices are in fact an enticement that almost invariably outweighs any sentimental attachment to the old homestead.

The first impact of speculative activity on the rural landscape is generally geared to the generation cycle. Father continues farming, much as Grandfather did, until retirement day. If Son has not already been lured away by the dazzle of the city, he now faces a grave choice: Should he continue the family tradition, knowing it will likely remain a hard-work, high-risk, low-return proposition, or should he give up a lost cause to eager speculators, knowing that profits made from turning fields and orchards into subdivisions or industrial parks are probably far greater than he can hope to earn by raising crops or livestock? Most often it is the dollar that decides, but either choice will show in the landscape.

This is the first shock wave of the advancing frontier; many more will follow. As they come rolling out across the landscape from their urban epicentre, they crumble the foundations of rural life, clearing the way for the final assault by the city. The change of ownership usually brings a change in crops and cropping methods. Family-operated mixed farming is replaced by corporate cash-cropping of corn or soyabeans. Fences are neglected or removed. A barn which recently housed Ol'Macdonald's menagerie now shelters a single age group of hogs or cattle. Eventually, even this becomes "too much trouble for what it's worth" and the barn stands empty and silent except for the chirping sparrows in the rafters. In time it is demolished, leaving only the foundation poking out of the weeds—until, at last, a bulldozer erases every trace.

The house, meanwhile, may be occupied by the original owners for a time, or it may be rented on a short-term basis. Such tenants develop no roots, knowing that their stay may be ended abruptly. (While living in such a house, I once quietly attended a Kitchener City Council meeting

Facing page: Brampton's frontier, Peel R. M., Aug. 21, 1983.

where a proposed condominium development for this property was discussed at length. The house was not mentioned once. Apparently, it had already ceased to exist in the minds of city councillors, developers, and even an opposing citizens' group from the subdivision across the street. The great irony was that, with a little maintenance, that fine old brick farmhouse could have outlasted every building in the neighbourhood. Needless to say, it didn't.) After the tenants leave, such a house may sit empty for months or even years. "No Trespassing" signs greet the passerby, and children say it's haunted. Suddenly one day it disappears in a cloud of dust. The former farmstead looks like a battlefield—a cratered and uninhabited wasteland.

A short distance down the road in the direction of the city, where the long-gone neighbours once farmed, the highway has been widened, and expanses of tinted plate glass and faceless brick walls echo the ebb and flow of ceaseless traffic. Everything is new; even the topography has been reshaped. Waves of rooftops come flooding over the horizon. New people come to live in new houses and work in new factories; they mow new lawns and water new trees; they wash new cars and relax in new swimming pools. Rarely do they stop to think of the men and horses who for generations plodded back and forth across fields which existed here so recently. This may be the same *location*, but it has become a new and different *place*.

A new suburb has no history. But then, neither did the now-forgotten farms when they were newly hacked out of the bush. There is no substitute for the passage of time.

In a country as vast as Canada it seems ironic that there could be any shortage of land, and yet around most cities competition for land has become a grave concern. The situation is closely watched by citizens' groups. And at both the municipal and provincial levels there are restrictions (some say "too lenient," others "too severe") which inhibit rampant urbanization.

Without controls and municipal planning, the frontier would hardly be identifiable as a continuous band. Instead, there would be a more widely scattered hodgepodge of urban development around our cities.

A large or rapidly growing city will have a broad and conspicuous frontier—a peripheral band of agricultural decline and decay. An expanding village may also have a frontier, but it might affect only one farm or parts of a few. Its advance will be much slower and less dramatic. Existing houses are far more likely to be incorporated with the new developments. While the loss of farmland to Ontario's villages is of little consequence,

conflicts with rural non-farm residents, usually over barnyard odours, are becoming more frequent.

Within the urban frontier of the larger cities, villages themselves are susceptible. In Metro Toronto, for example, there are numerous place-names derived from villages now entirely absorbed by the metropolis: e.g. Islington, Weston, Swansea, Yorkville, Davisville, Leaside, Don Mills, and Westhill. Other villages have disappeared without leaving so much as a name.

Cities grow and grow. But what drives their relentless expansion? Who are the pioneers on the urban frontier?

Roughly eighty percent of Canadians now live in urban areas; a century ago the same percentage was rural. A steady migration from farms to cities has taken place, and at the same time the majority of new Canadians have settled in the larger urban centres. Like cities around the world, the magnetism of our urban centres is proportional to their size.

Within our cities there also has been a significant migration from the inner core to the suburbs. The movement began as an escape from the aging and congested housing in downtown areas, and continues today as the popular alternative to high-rise apartments and the now fashionably renewed, and expensive, downtown districts.

But the people who come to live in a new subdivision are not its true pioneers. They have not created the new environment, but merely occupy it. Their arrival signals the passing of the frontier. With few exceptions, the urban frontier is pioneered by corporate entities. Economy of scale dictates that capital be pooled, and that the work of building transportation networks, water and sewage systems, housing projects, shopping malls, and industrial parks be divided among specialists. And so the true pioneers are paper entities—development companies representing a host of contractors and subcontractors from surveyors to sod layers.

Very little of a former agricultural landscape survives the frontier. But those few elements which do survive are quite often sanctified and enshrined as "designated heritage." Their value in the placeless vacuum that surrounds them is quickly recognized. If the events on the frontier were governed more directly by the people who eventually occupy these new places, perhaps old landscapes would be coaxed and molded into new urban uses. "Paradise" might stand a chance of being recognized for what it is *before* it gets paved over for a parking lot. Continuity in the landscape may not count for much in a corporate boardroom, but it is central to community spirit.

APR 21, 1984 / APR 30, 1986

57. The urban frontier is a prime natural habitat for most species of earthmovers, bulldozers, and backhoes. Because they are so disruptive of their environment, they tend to migrate with the advancing frontier. Unmistakable evidence of their recent presence is seen here on the north edge of Waterloo, where the city spills out over what had been superb farmland.

58. Nearby, signs of the city-to-come are replaced by the landscape of the city itself. In the distance farm buildings are being razed. Much can happen in just two years.

59. A view from the banks of the Grand River looks east toward Breslau and southeast toward Kitchener. There is no hint of the city in the circa 1945 scene; Kitchener is still three miles (5 km) and four decades away.

Today, the urban frontier is advancing from right to left across this scene. On the near side of Highway 7, a farm has been completely leveled. Across the road the buildings remain intact, but in less than one year they too will vanish. For a short time the landscape is a battleground, a no-man's-land; and then, inevitably, it becomes part of the city.

60. Nowhere is the urban frontier wider or more thoroughly destructive of past landscapes than around our largest city. Toronto has an insatiable appetite for farmland. And yet near West Hill, now part of Scarborough, a bit of rural scenery has escaped the usual fate. It stands like an island in an urban sea. The one-room school is gone, but the site is marked by a plaque which states: "In memory of Lucy Sevanton Doyle, 1880-1971. Noted newspaper woman... owned the schoolhouse built here in 1870. Her cherished wish was that her 'valley' become part of Scarborough College grounds." With only minor changes, the buildings and the grounds are now used for administrative residences and recreational facilities. Although the main advance has been turned aside, the possibility will always remain that this bit of old West Hill might be overrun by a highway project or some other use.

61. Baden, a village in Waterloo Region, has a narrow frontier in keeping with its small size. There are a few new houses strung out along the main road and some around the periphery. Their backyards face fields that seem destined to be subdivided. But it also appears that, in general, the trees are growing faster than the village!

SEPT 12, 1984 / J. BOYD OCT 1, 1916 / PUBLIC ARCHIVES CANADA PA-69945

62. From 1000 feet (300 m) above Hamilton Harbour, these views to the south show 59 years of urban expansion on land which has become the eastern part of Hamilton. Parkdale Avenue and Burlington Street are prominent. In 1927, a relatively narrow band of urban sprawl marked the advancing frontier at the edge of the city, but today it has pushed far to the east of this view.

63. By 1971, the 1954 pattern of these fields northeast of Richmond Hill (York R.M.) had been all but obliterated. Conversion swept from left to right—a subdivision, a golf course, a gravel pit, and the beginnings of yet another subdivision. A small creek has been partially confined to a "rationalized" channel, but at least some of the woodlots on its banks appear destined to survive as parklands. The scale is approximately 1:16,500.

64-5. In 1954, at Dixon Road (Borough of Etobicoke, Toronto) Highway 401 was under construction through a landscape still dominated by farms. The change in only fifteen years is mind-boggling.

66. Headon Forest, a housing development in Burlington, illustrates the final stage in the transition from rural to urban land use. One year has brought about an amazing change in the landscape—but it hasn't exactly changed a moonscape into a forest. Euphemisms for housing projects, such as "forest," "village," or "park," are universally applied and accepted. The concocted names help to give a little sense of place and identity to mass-produced landscapes that are inherently placeless.

67. On the edge of Waterloo, this farmhouse was saved from probable destruction when converted to a nursing home in 1964. A small chapel has been built where the barn once stood.

In the foreground, row-house foundations begun by the Greymac Corporation are rapidly being overtaken by weeds just a few months after the provincial government froze the company's assets. Vandalism quickly set in on the site, apparently reflecting the resentment of nearby single-family housing residents who opposed low-cost town houses in their neighbourhood. The buildings were, however, eventually completed.

AUG 20, 1983

SEPT 8, 1984

SEPT 24, 1983 / W. J. TOPLEY 1913 PAC PA-10914

68. In 1913, this barnyard was two miles (3 km) down the road from Woodstock, a small town in the heart of Canada's foremost dairy country. Today, the frontier is here. Little remains of the barnyard. Already there are a few factories in the neighbourhood and more are inevitable. The present landscape is in an eclipsed phase: a landscape that waits. Who notices or cares about the concrete ruins and barnyard relics that lie hidden among the weeds?

69. It so happened that a farm down the road toward Woodstock once produced a world champion dairy cow. Some years after this 1913 photo was taken, Springbank Snow Countess broke all previous records for butterfat production, bringing fame to her owner, Thomas R. Dent, and to the community of Woodstock. A monument commemorating this remarkable Holstein was erected a year after the Countess died. In a parkette beside the road we find this unusual reminder that the land here was a farm not so long ago.

The old rural highway is being torn up to be remade as a city street. Alternating mud and dust are a temporary reminder of its long history as a dirt road.

CHAPTER FOUR

Hamlets and Villages

ALEXANDRIA, Athens, Baltimore, Boston, Brussels, Cankerville, Copenhagen, Damascus, Delhi, Dogs Nest, Dresden, Hanover, Heidelberg, Lisbon, London, Mannheim, Moscow, Paris, Perth, Punkeydoodles Corners, Salem, Sparta, Troy, Utopia, Vienna, Washington, and Zurich—What do they have in common?

They can all be found in Southern Ontario. Most, of course, are tiny places of no great consequence to the world as a whole. But a few have grown to become towns, and London is the fourth largest city in the province. The borrowed names are a reminder of the many, varied sources of the province's cultural mosaic.

Virtually every urban place in Ontario began as a hamlet—a product of the mutual efforts and aspirations of a handful of people. In the frontier days of Upper Canada everyone was an immigrant and a stranger; the need to identify with a community was particularly acute. Whether a fort, mill, inn, store, or church provided the nucleus, what mattered was a personal centre of focus, a comfortable sense of place, and a feeling of belonging.

Hamlets and villages by the hundreds sprang up to meet the social and economic needs of an insular population. The problem of isolation was most severe in the early days, however, and it gradually diminished. Places which seemed widely separated when they were established now seem very close.

Improvements in transportation and communications have eroded the importance of most small places in Southern Ontario. For example, while larger centres benefited from the building of the railroads, only a small percentage of the many hamlets and villages were directly on the rail lines, and of these only some found it to be to their advantage. The rest were undermined.

Rerouted commerce has halted the growth of many small places and abandoned stores and factories have long been common sights. A decline in population inevitably follows, but this happens more slowly. After several generations have developed deep roots, it may take protracted hardship to cause families to start new lives elsewhere. Most often it is the young people who move. Seeing few opportunities close to home, they head for a nearby growing town or city.

Like the "boom and bust" of northern mining towns, many of Southern Ontario's hamlets and villages have experienced the elation of rapid growth and the despair of the slow slide toward oblivion. As a rule, the saga is played out more gradually in the south, but the landscapes contain many shared elements. Sagging roof lines, tilted door jambs, and patchwork renovations often indicate which buildings were put up in haste and which will be the first to be abandoned. Boarded or broken windows, unmowed lawns, heaving sidewalks, and faded "For Sale" signs are very much a part of such scenes. Landscapes of decline and poverty, though often unnoticed, are scattered all across the province and can be found in any rural county.

The smaller a place is, the more it will depend on its agricultural hinterland for its continued existence. Therefore, decline has been the fate of many hamlets, but villages have generally fared better. While villages too have lost much of their importance in the central place system, many have recently begun to profit from a growing influx of urban tourists. This new economy fits well with the popular image of the village as a tranquil, almost static, place that never suffers the extremes of growth or decline. At times this new niche can also be at odds with the traditional economic and social functions of these places, though it may not be obvious to a casual visitor.

Facing page: Winterbourne, Waterloo R.M., Aug. 11, 1986.

This chapter, and the two following, somewhat loosely divide urban places into rather arbitrary categories based on their municipal status as of 1981. From a small cluster of houses to a world class metropolis, this region offers every example, and lines drawn between them are necessarily artificial. A few generalities might be useful, however. The population of most villages falls between 300 and 2000, while towns range upward to 15,000 and more. Cities require 10,000 inhabitants in order to incorporate, and most are considerably larger. It could be argued, too, by another definition of what a city is, that Toronto is alone in this class.

At the small end of the scale, a hamlet could be thought of as a place with more than one house, but not big enough to call itself anything else. Together hamlets and villages far outnumber towns and cities. But these places are so small that only about one percent of Southern Ontario's population actually lives in them.

Many Ontarians, however, have some real or sentimental connection with hamlets and villages, just as they do with farms. From these ties flow some widely held notions about life in a village. On one hand, it is upheld as an idyllic kind of place where big city crime and grime are unknown, and life goes on with very little stress or hardship. On the other hand, such an existence is felt to be so lacking in stimulation that it would be quite intolerable to anyone accustomed to city life. Perhaps there is an element of truth in these opinions, but they are hardly shared by the villagers themselves.

People living in small communities tend to have a stronger affinity for their locale than their urban cousins. Their identity and self-esteem are very much caught up in the life of their community. And the community derives a large measure of its character directly from the individuals who inhabit it. Everybody knows everybody, intertwined family relationships are common, and to a degree the community operates like one family. Rivalry, peer pressure, and gossip are often rampant, but at the same time mutual concern and assistance flow more freely than in larger centres.

In the village landscape, subtle relationships between people and their property are reflected in the pattern and distribution of such things as hedges, abandoned cars, lawn ornaments, dandelions, and flower beds. Shade trees, outbuildings, sidewalks, and gable trim are all part of the local history as well as being familiar, integral parts of the lives of the residents. These landscape elements are not static, of course, but the rate of change is slow enough to permit comfortable assimilation. Even the signs and posters plastered across the front windows of the General Store seldom change; they gradually become invisible, fading in the sunlight as their messages and their very presence fade into the subconscious.

The outward appearance of a hamlet or village can never be the same for a stranger as for an inhabitant. The perceptions of a long-time resident will be tempered by familiarity and coloured by insights and oversights that arise, more or less unconsciously, from the blending of the physical landscape with its social counterpart.

Newcomers to a typical village or hamlet are likely to be greeted with a cheerful welcome—and a closed society. They will probably move on before long. It takes time to become integrated. But those who do, like those who have lived there always, are likely to speak of their community with civic pride and with the confidence that in all the world there is no better place to live.

73. Bond Head is a crossroads community about halfway between Toronto and Barrie. This view is to the east, looking down Highway 88 from Highway 27. Both roads were formerly of greater importance. Highway 27 lost its role as a major north-south artery to the "400." The road now known as Highway 88 once linked the area with the water transport routes of Lake Simcoe. In the 1850s, the six miles (10 km) between Bond Head and Bradford were completely covered with heavy planks. This made a fine road, but maintenance costs were very high and by the time this photo was taken the planks had already been removed.

Today, many cars pass through Bond Head each day, but very few stop; there are few businesses here. Although a few new buildings have replaced some of those in the 1860 photo, there was virtually no real growth for a century. Recent decades have seen some new housing as the hamlet becomes a Toronto "bedroom community."

The building on the extreme right is readily recognizable; on the left, the corner store appears relatively unchanged, but is it really the same building?

74. Silver Water, on western Manitoulin Island, was a lively, if somewhat dispersed, rural community in the 1920s. But the shallow soils prevented farmers from participating in progressive, twentieth-century agriculture. The sign in front of the community hall announces that there is still a spark of life here today, but abandoned houses and barns are at least as common as those still occupied. This dramatic depopulation of the countryside has undercut any business prospects in Silver Water. Only a general store survives, and it has not changed much in fifty years.

75. Lonsdale (Hastings Co.) began to flourish in the mid-nineteenth century when the Salmon River was harnessed to power various mills. Numerous businesses and homes grew up around this nucleus. But by the end of the century the lack of a railroad and the distance to markets was making Lonsdale's industries uncompetitive. A long, slow decline set in. One of the mills already had been reduced to a shell in the 1908 photo. Today, another of the mills has been converted to a residence. A few other homes, including the stately house at the end of the street, are still occupied, but otherwise Lonsdale is truly a ghost town.

76. Mountain View (Prince Edward Co.) was imaginatively named—there is no mountain, and although there once was a view from this vantage point, it has since been lost behind a wall of trees.

The hamlet has not changed much over the years. The building at the intersection lost its verandah, but the church, not surprisingly, is unchanged. A close inspection of the old photo reveals maple leaf ornamentation on the fence and gate that enclose the cemetery. Amazingly, these leaves still survive. Such fencing was once very popular but is now virtually extinct, having fallen victim to rust and changing fashions. A carefully maintained coat of paint protects this one.

77. Lowville (Halton R.M.) is beautifully situated in a valley between the Niagara Escarpment and Mount Nemo (centre background). Several mills, such as the one in the lower right corner (now a residence), prompted the development of this small community on Bronte Creek. But these industries shared the fate of hundreds of others across the province—improved roads, railroads, changing technology, and cheap electricity brought stiff competition, and only the fittest survived.

78

SEPT 14, 1983

78-9. For one hundred years, Benmiller (Huron Co.) prospered as a centre for flour milling and other farm-related industries. After the mill shut down, the beautiful setting attracted an entrepreneur who has developed an inn and related facilities here. At the very moment the 1983 picture was taken, Premier William Davis and his "Big Blue Machine" were secluded in the old mill (obscured by trees near the centre of the photo), while reporters swarmed around the front entrance.

The inset shows the actual point of view, while the larger photo is from the best available vantage point (the ridge on the left in the older view).

80. Only a few buildings have been replaced in the downtown section of Neustadt (Grey Co.). Even the second-floor balconies on the general store have survived. The most notable change, aside from the replacement of horse-drawn vehicles by cars and trucks, is, once again, the growth of trees. Unlike most previous scenes in this chapter, the trees here were planted.

81. Enniskillen (Durham R. M.) already had a pleasantly shaded main street in the early 1900s. A new generation of maples now graces the street, perpetuating the serene atmosphere of the village despite the fact that, at least in this view, there has been a dramatic change in architectural detail.

MARY ANNE ROBERTS / CA 1910 / (?) / SEPT 9, 1983

CA 1905   Wm. WEBER   /   (?)

CA 1916   Wm. WEBER   /   (?)

OCT 28, 1983   /

82

82. Looking northeast from a hill on the edge of Erin (Wellington Co.), the large stone building at the centre of the view is McMillan's grist mill, built in 1834. It was powered by water channeled through a penstock which runs under the main street.

The oldest photo shows hotels on either side of the mill. On the right, the Queen's Hotel (the long, narrow building) was destroyed by fire in 1913. It has been replaced by other buildings in the 1916 photo. To the left of the mill, the Globe Hotel was busy from its founding in 1866 until 1945, when it too was destroyed by fire.

83. Hopetown, a small community in Lanark County, sprang up around a nucleus of small mills. Although there is some good farmland in the area, there is not enough to sustain more than a few basic services here.

The hill from which the photos were taken has been partially removed for its gravel. Nearby, the fence seems to be down to its last rails.

84. The old hotel in Norwood (Peterborough Co.) was used as a warehouse in 1983. But the boarded windows foreshadowed its demise and it has since gone the way of the other buildings on the block. Despite the tremendous increase in traffic through this village, local merchants benefit only a little. The cars and trucks are mostly going elsewhere, and the residents, too, are inclined to do their shopping down the highway. Some teenagers on nearby steps watched with barely concealed curiosity as I took my picture. When I showed them the circa 1920 photo, they were quite amazed. "Not much there now," one of them mused.

85ab. The Dominion Hotel in St. Jacobs (Waterloo R.M.) is as old as the village. When the business was begun in 1852, it was called the Farmer's Inn. It has served a local clientele as well as travellers ever since. Although horses and buggies are still commonly seen in the village today, things have changed. Horses must still wait outside the hotel, but some now get to ride through the village!

85cd. The strikingly similar Dominion House in Vankleek Hill (Prescott & Russell Co.) dates from 1857. The building is now occupied by a dry goods store (presumably no pun intended) and a men's wear store.

CA 1920   PAC C-27214

AUG 1, 1983   /   (?)

CA 1880 / (?) MARVIN C. SMITH

JAN 4, 1983 / (?)

ND ST-GREGOIRE--ST.GREGORY VANKLEEK HILL 1878-1978

JUNE 29, 1983 / (?)

GRAND BEND

THE
TENDER
SPOT

GARDEN CENTRE
SIDE O' PORK .99 lb
BEEF SALE SIDES 1.59
FRONT 1.39 LB
HIND 1.99 lb

THE TENDER SPOT

GOLDEN PALACE
FINE DINING

86. Grand Bend, on Lake Huron, began to develop as a resort during the 1890s. The village is situated on the boundary between Huron and Lambton Counties, and originally was part of Huron, but it joined Lambton when Huron elected to remain dry after the repeal of the *Temperance Act*. To stay with Huron would have been detrimental to the tourist trade.

On the main street of Grand Bend, a long-established grocery store has expanded piecemeal, in every direction, so that it now takes a close look to see the original building. The store serves a permanent community of 750 residents, but on summer weekends the population can swell to an estimated 20,000 fun seekers.

87. A few miles south of Sarnia's "Chemical Valley" is the village of Corunna with its wide, western-style main street. This view is to the south, toward the main intersection; however, the exact location of the Corunna Hotel was not determined. Is the restaurant a renovated hotel? No one seems to know.

87

88. Occasionally, change comes to a village in a revolutionary fashion. This was the case in Iroquois when in the mid-1950s the village was relocated to make way for the new St. Lawrence Seaway and its associated hydro-electric development. Over 150 homes were carefully lifted from their foundations and moved to the new town site. Others were demolished, along with the entire downtown area. The "new" village has no downtown—only a plaza which looked wonderfully modern when it opened.

89ab. At Queenston, on the Niagara River, changes have come as though the clock was running backward. Laura Secord, the young heroine of the War of 1812, lived here at the time of the American invasion. By 1925, her home had been considerably renovated. Its importance as a historic site, however, had long been recognized (note the stone marker), and eventually the building was restored to appear as it did in the 1840s.

89cd. Paisley (Bruce Co.) is a small community picturesquely located on the Saugeen River. Its stately town hall, which dates from 1876, had fallen into disrepair and was in danger of going the way of the town scales. Instead, it was carefully restored to become the area's premier architectural showpiece.

AUG 1925   PAC PA-26898

(?)

AUG 26, 1983

ND   BRUCE COUNTY MUSEUM 958.174.5

(?)

AUG 14, 1983

TOWN SCALES

CHAPTER FIVE

Towns

IN MANY instances, the building of a pioneer enterprise—a mill, store, inn, or blacksmith shop perhaps—encouraged complementary businesses to establish nearby. Employment opportunities created a demand for housing. And housing, besides creating jobs in the building trades, meant the expansion of secondary services and industries which required even more buildings. Where conditions were right, this kind of cyclic growth could soon turn a village into a town—a bustling, self-important hub of commercial activity, or, to paraphrase the directories of the day, "the biggest and the busiest place for miles around."

Despite its urban pretensions, even a large Southern Ontario town in the era before cars would seem very rural by today's standards. Along muddy streets flanked by boardwalks, the homes and yards would look more like crowded farmsteads, without the intervening fields. Behind many houses was a small stable where a horse or team was kept to provide family transportation. A cow or other livestock was only a little less likely than in a village, and daily chores were nearly as much a part of life in town as in the country.

Aside from their size, the difference between towns and villages was most evident in their downtowns. As a general rule, a town would have at least a block solidly built up with three-storey structures, whereas in a village a more discontinuous section of two-storey buildings typically predominated. The distinction is still useful today.

The business districts of many towns grew rapidly during the railroad era. The automobile, however, sapped the vitality of most towns within easy driving distance of larger centres. In this century, adequate existing commercial space has meant relatively little new development. Slow growth has had a preservative effect on the architectural heritage of many Ontario towns.

Since reasonably well-preserved Victorian facades are common throughout Ontario, one "Main Street" tends to look much like any other. No doubt this reflects the fabled conservatism of the Canadian entrepreneur; but perhaps a more important key to explaining the striking similarities of so many buildings and downtowns has to do with fire.

In the early days, building codes were nonexistent, lumber was cheap and bricks were scarce, and heat was supplied by wood- or coal-burning stoves. There was an ever-present danger of fire and, at the same time, fire protection was hopelessly inadequate. Nineteenth-century newspapers frequently carried vivid accounts of conflagrations that destroyed entire blocks or business districts. The replacement of these losses happened more or less quickly, which produced a coherent architectural style. The new buildings showed greater heed to the fire hazard, being usually built of brick and incorporating many fire protection features.

The nineteenth-century facades lining Main Street contrast sharply with modern signs and storefronts at street level. Modernization seldom extends to the second and third storeys. Except for the disappearance of ostentatious details, the upper storeys mostly appear unchanged. You can learn much about a town's history by simply looking up!

In recent decades, many towns near our larger cities are being transformed by unprecedented growth and prosperity. Their original nuclei are completely overwhelmed and displaced by peripheral shopping malls, industrial parks, and neighbourhood plazas. And community spirit, too, is diffused as much business, recreation, and social activity tends to be drawn toward the nearby city.

In sharp contrast, other towns have learned to capitalize on their Victorian quaintness by drawing tourists from the cities. No doubt, there are many more towns that are just beginning to wake up to this potential.

Facing page: 10th Street, Hanover, Grey Co., Oct. 1, 1984.

(?)   JUNE 30, 1978   MINISTRY OF NATURAL RESOURCES 78.4406 135-39   /   (?)   1966   MNR 66-4404 101-74

92. Shelburne (Dufferin Co.), a typical Southern Ontario town of 3,000, grew substantially during the prosperous 1960s and 1970s, after a long period of dormancy. The downtown area, however, remains relatively unchanged, as most growth took place on the outskirts of town. The large complex near the upper edge of the photos is a home for the elderly. The scale of these vertical photos is approximately 1:9,500, and south is at the top.

93. Grimsby has been transformed from a rural village to a large suburban town. A close examination of these photos reveals much about how this came about. The basic pattern of the village remains relatively unchanged in today's town—the local road network is still evident—but superimposed on it is a new pattern with regional and provincial characteristics. In the late 1930s, the first of Ontario's superhighways was built. The Queen Elizabeth Way has had a profound effect on the growth of Grimsby. This fast, convenient link with Hamilton has greatly spurred development, but at the same time it also has made the town a virtual suburb of its larger neighbour.

94. On the south shore of Georgian Bay, the lovely town of Meaford presents a typical downtown scene from the pre-automobile era—two and three storey buildings, decorated with ornate brickwork, overlook an elevated boardwalk and a dirt roadway. On the right, many architectural details have survived, particularly at the second storey level, although some false roof lines have been removed. On the left, some of the buildings were destroyed by fire.

95. Cobourg, on Lake Ontario, was first known as Burkville, then as Amherst, and then Hamilton, before its present name was adopted in 1819. Its geographic location led many to believe that the port of Cobourg could become a rival of Kingston, Toronto, and Hamilton. And there were dreams of becoming the capital of Upper Canada. In a bid to further such ambitions, a preposterous town hall (its tower is visible near the centre of the photos) was built between 1856 and 1860. By the early 1970s, Victoria Hall had become structurally unsound and it narrowly escaped demolition. Today, thanks to the efforts of concerned citizens, this landmark stands fully restored. The building on the right was originally an armoury, and is now the local police headquarters.

ND   MEAFORD MUSEUM   (?)   /   JUNE 20, 1983

J. C. SMITH   OCT 9, 1896   RIDGETOWN HISTORICAL SOCIETY   /   SEPT 2, 1983

J. C. SMITH   SEPT 25, 1896   R. H. S.   /   SEPT 2, 1983

J. C. SMITH / CA 1900   B. (JIM) SMITH   SEPT 2, 1983

A sign at the edge of a town in the southwest corner of the province reads: "Welcome to Ridgetown—The friendliest town in Ontario." Corn fields give way to tree-lined streets and comfortable, neat and tidy homes built in the late 1800s. Once a railway boom town, today it is a quiet town of 3,500. "Almost too quiet," a policeman commented.

From the main intersection, set squarely in the centre of town, the entire downtown area displays remarkable architectural harmony. There are no glaring nonconformities; no garish commercialism screaming for dominance. Everywhere the atmosphere is genuinely relaxed. Nowhere is there evidence of great wealth, nor real poverty.

Pleasant—no single word better describes Ridgetown. The residents certainly have an exceptionally keen interest in the town's history and architectural heritage, and it is not mere chance that this congenial environment is preserved. Is it the pleasantness of the surroundings that makes the folks so friendly?

96. Looking east (above) and west on Main St. from Erie St.

97. 41 Erie St. S. (built 1880).

98-9. 18 Broadway (built 1897); 110 Main St. E.; 50 Main St. W.; and 25 York St. E. (built c.1875).

97

100. The main street of Wingham (Bruce Co.) has seen a few changes, but the size of the downtown area appears to have remained much the same since the turn of the century. The railroad did not arrive here in time to make a great impact on the town's rate of growth.

However, as a communications centre, Wingham has achieved regional importance. With a population of less than 3,000, it is the smallest community in Canada to boast its own television station and production facilities. There is a radio station here as well.

The castle-like "Bank of Hamilton" is now protected as a Heritage Building. Perhaps the bank across the street might also be protected today, if the success of the company had not led to the building's early replacement.

101. Twenty miles (32 km) to the southeast, Listowel has a population of 5,000. But its downtown is only about the same size as Wingham's. Listowel is closer to large urban centres which tend to siphon away consumer dollars and commercial development. On the left, where the imposing Post Office once stood, a forlorn vacant lot attempts to lure a new enterprise with a sign that is beginning to look like a permanent fixture.

ALLAN D. MacKINNON (?) CA 1925 / JUNE 29, 1983

102. Gore Bay, on Manitoulin Island, is rather isolated from the rest of Ontario, especially during the winter months. But this isolation enhances its local importance. Although only the size of a village, this town is the administrative centre for the world's largest freshwater island.

On Gore Bay's waterfront, the prominent Queen's Hotel is now a residence. The ubiquitous board fences protected private property in the days when livestock was driven through the streets to the docks. The older photo was taken from a hill which has since been excavated for its gravel.

103. Fifty miles (80 km) east of Ottawa, the Main Street of Vankleek Hill displays an eclectic array of architectural gems and curiosities. But the most striking characteristic is the many multi-storey verandahs, well maintained and invariably painted white. In this thoroughly bilingual town, their preservation is primarily a reflection of French-Canadian culture. The tendency for domestic life to spill out into the street makes the verandah an ideal interface between private and public facets of life.

103

104. Looking west from John Street, downtown Napanee's Dundas Street looks much as it did at the turn of the century. A few windows have been bricked in, most of the cornices have been modified, and an entirely new crop of signs greets the shopper's eye, but essentially the architecture remains unchanged.

The telephone wires, which appear as conspicuous eyesores to us, were once a readily accepted part of the landscape. Their practical value as a link with the rest of the world even gave some beauty to such lines. Their ugliness was unmasked only when new technology made them obsolete. Perhaps some day people will feel the same about the cars parked on the street!

105. Two hundred and twenty miles (352 km) to the west, in Bruce County, Southampton's broad main street provides a view of Lake Huron. The community grew up around a natural harbour at the mouth of the Saugeen River where fur traders were established well before agricultural settlement began. Lumbering and fishing were important in the early days, and furniture became big business later. Today, tourism is a major industry.

ND   LENNOX & ADDINGTON COUNTY MUSEUM 225   AUG 2, 1984   /   (?)

1905   (?)   /   OCT 13, 1983

106. Foster Street in Perth (Lanark Co.) is part of a lively shopping district which is more extensive than might be expected in a town of 5,000. With a wide hinterland of many lakes and rivers, tourism is important and growing.

Heritage Canada selected Perth as a pilot project for its Main Street Program, offering technical advice and assistance to merchants wishing to restore or upgrade their properties. Although there was initial skepticism, the community soon agreed that a coordinated approach to street planning made economic as well as aesthetic sense.

107. In Wellington County, Fergus competes with several larger urban centres, and its business district is noticeably smaller than Perth's, even though it has a slightly larger population. Like Perth, Fergus has an architectural heritage of limestone buildings.

On the extreme right, the shell of the old town hall became the centre of a long and bitter struggle between the church next door, which wanted the building demolished, and an ad hoc committee of residents intent on its preservation. The 1983 photo shows a court injunction affixed to the front door, temporarily staying the wrecker's ball. But it was to no avail; today there is a parking lot in its place.

107

CHAPTER SIX

Cities

To the modern eye, turn-of-the-century cityscapes combined elegance with litter and clutter. Horse buns and gawky telephone poles were as commonplace then as exhaust fumes and traffic lights are today. Such landscape elements remain tolerable and, in an aesthetic sense, unnoticed, until new technology makes them conspicuously obsolete.

Cities have been slowly evolving over many thousands of years, but until recent centuries their size and complexity was severely limited by a lack of progress in sanitation, transportation, and architectural innovation. Ontario's cities developed during a time of major advances in these areas.

Garbage, sewage, pollution, slums and other obsolete landscapes have contributed more to the development of the city than they are generally given credit for. Today's urban environment is cleaner and healthier than ever before, but it should be noted that the shining modern city came about in response to growing public intolerance for urban meanness. And the perception of meanness, to reiterate, depends considerably on the alternatives that technology can provide.

Technology—the steam engine, gasoline engine, and electricity—set in motion the building of the modern city. Street cars and trains, and then cars and trucks, moved people and goods to, from, and through the city in unprecedented volume. At the same time, stationary engines, electric motors, lights, and telephones promoted mass production and consolidation.

Technology drew the basic outline of our modern cityscapes with bigger and taller buildings. Steel and concrete provided the structural strength, and elevators provided transportation for vertical expansion. Not surprisingly, Victorian styles were at first incorporated with the fantastic new technological possibilites. But when plate glass came to be rec-

ognized as the ideal outer skin, a radical new school of architecture—the Bauhaus or International style—came into vogue.

"Glass box" architecture carries a trademark emphasis on functionalism and the complete absence of decoration. Undeniably, this has produced many stark and decidedly ugly buildings. Perhaps, however, the cityscape has been saved from an even worse fate. If architecture had followed its established traditions, might the new materials and techniques have filled our cities with outrageously expensive and grotesquely ornate monstrosities?

As the pendulum swung radically toward utter blandness, the older city, reflected in shimmering expanses of glass, was made to look still older and much of it crumbled under the wrecker's ball. But then, inevitably, against a rising tide of public outrage and dismay, the sanitizing sweep of the new style began to lose momentum.

Like a dandelion springing up through pavement, the idea of heritage preservation has made its way to the forefront of urban planning in recent decades. A revival of appreciation for older architectural styles is becoming evident in new construction as well. From town houses to skyscrapers, a refreshing renaissance of humanizing, decorative aesthetics appears to be rapidly gaining acceptance.

While urban architecture has changed considerably over time, its distinctiveness from one place to another continues to decline. Today's styles are cosmopolitan; thus, most building projects are drawn from an increasingly homogeneous pool of ideas, and only the largest centres can afford to build unique and innovative landmarks.

There is perhaps no better example of such a landmark than Toronto's CN Tower—a tower for the sake of a tower, and a concrete, science fiction counterpart to Monsieur Eiffel's pinnacle of steel.

Facing page: King and University, Toronto, Apr, 26, 1984.

FISHER (NORTHWAY)   JUNE 12, 1978   MINISTRY OF NATURAL RESOURCES 78-4346 14-50   /   D. BENNETT   AUG 21, 1954   MNR 54-4330 23-153

110. Toronto resembles a crowded circuit board in these vertical photographs from 1954 and 1978. The component list includes thousands of cars, buildings, sidewalks, lawns, and even trees. In Queen's Park, the trees are doing very well. Elsewhere, large new buildings now dominate, particularly where the central core area has spilled into the neighbourhood of City Hall (top centre).

111. Market Street in Brantford was named for a block of open space (now a parking lot, just to the right of the photo) which once hosted a weekly farmers' market. Across the street, every building has been replaced in this century. Gone, too, are the hundreds of wires—once a special source of pride for the Telephone City. Despite modernization, downtown Brantford has considerable vacant commercial space.

112-3. In sharp contrast, Stratford has a healthy downtown, helped considerably by the fame of the Stratford Festival. An annual influx of people and money staves off the decay that plagues so many North American cities.

The irregular street pattern does little for traffic flow, but it greatly enhances the city's atmosphere by creating partially hidden vistas which invite exploration.

111

114-5. As in most Ontario towns and cities, the banks in Owen Sound have clustered around the main intersection. These views of 2nd Avenue East show that during the late 1920s there were impressive banks on all four corners. Today, the banks are as prominent as ever, but three of the buildings have been replaced, while the fourth has been renovated.

The older buildings were in harmony with the architectural style of the street. But the replacements, with their exotic designs, draw attention to themselves by invoking an image of efficiency and prosperity. In the process, they make the remainder of the block look old-fashioned. Sometimes the new buildings mimic details of the existing streetscape, as illustrated by the Toronto Dominion's bold scallops which mock the rounded casements of neighbouring buildings.

Owen Sound is no exception. In Southern Ontario, very few of the grand old bank buildings remain. It seems odd that the big banks, noted for their conservatism, should choose to be architecturally eccentric. But perhaps it is, after all, a fitting expression of the ruthless power of great stacks of money.

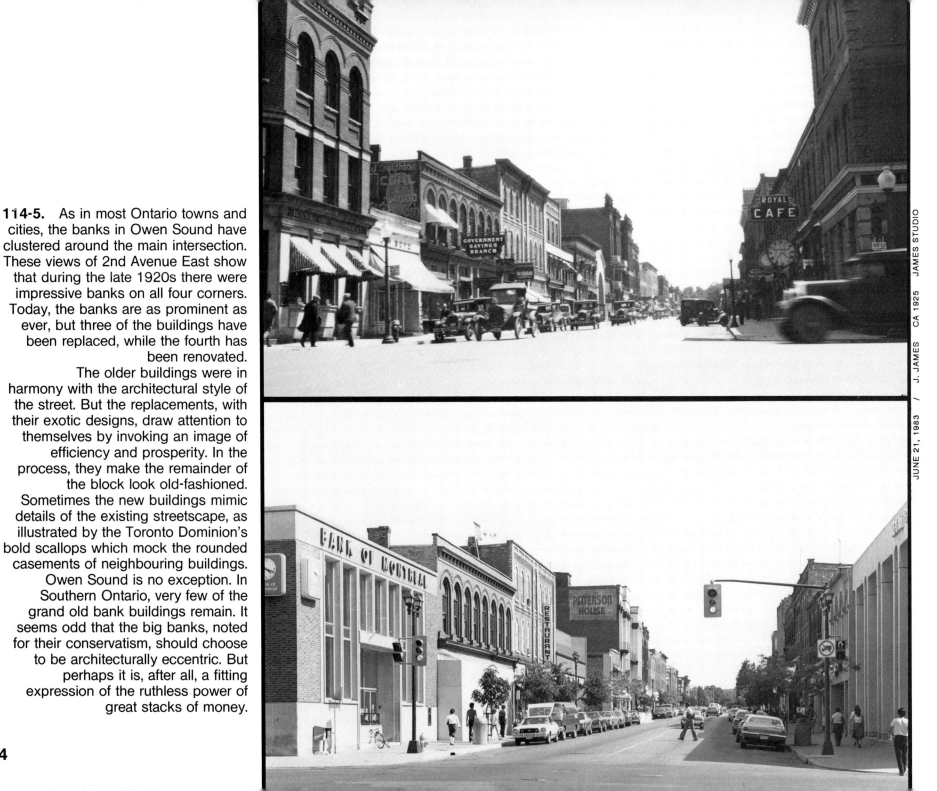

CA 1925 / J. JAMES JAMES STUDIO

JUNE 21, 1983

116. George Street as seen from Charlotte Street in Peterborough has been completely remade in the past 80 years, although a few of the "new" buildings predate the International Style of architecture. On the far right is a fine example of Beaux Arts elegance, while on the far left the more severe geometry of squares and horizontal lines identifies a touch of Art Deco design.

117. By the early 1970s it was apparent that Chatham's downtown was in trouble. The proliferation of shopping malls on the perimeter of the city was sucking the life out of the core area. The solution? Urban renewal, of course. The phrase has become as familiar as the pat solution—widened, bricked sidewalks; pedestrian crosswalks; benches; dressed-up garbage cans; planters full of petunias; and, invariably, exotic trees down both sides of the street.

Looking from the east end of King Street, a small park has replaced a magnificent Canadian Pacific hotel.

118-9. Urban renewal is generally helped along by a multi-million dollar redevelopment project (i.e., a mall) involving one or more large stores and many smaller shops. In this view from the west end of Chatham's downtown, the project is partially visible behind trees on the right.

117

When the sun set, the nineteenth-century city grew dark—pitch black when the moon did not shine. Late in the century, gas lights lit major intersections, but there was no street lighting as we think of it. At night, the city slept.

120. On the evening of November 22, 1911, electric street lights were turned on for the first time along King Street, Waterloo. Adam Beck declared that it was "the best-lighted town in Canada." In 1955, these lights were superseded by modern overhead lights. But now these too have been replaced with lights that look not unlike those installed in 1911, demonstrating that, even in street lighting, fashion is a cyclic thing!

121. Princess Street, Kingston, shows how the marvel of "hydro" had turned night into day. Note that virtually all the light came from street lights, whereas today the light originates mostly from store fronts and signs.

122-3. From the earliest times, Windsor has been overshadowed by Detroit, its giant neighbour directly across the river. In the past decade or two, high-rise developments have helped to give this city of 200,000 a measure of self-esteem and an air of sophistication.

Ouelette Avenue presents yet another urban renewal streetscape—definitely an improvement, though hardly original.

OH HP-1119 / NOV 22, 1911 / (?) / ONTARIO HYDRO HP-1120 / NOV 19, 1955 / (?) / DEC 13, 1984

(?) CA 1880 GUELPH CIVIC MUSEUM 975.21.96

(?) CA 1900 WELLINGTON COUNTY MUSEUM AND ARCHIVES ph3389

(?) CA 1925 GUELPH CIVIC MUSEUM 977.33.27

AUG 1986

124-5. St. George's Square is at the hub of Guelph, a planned city founded by John Galt in 1827. Until 1873, the centre of the square was dominated by St. George's Anglican Church, which was then replaced by the edifice that appears in each of the photos. The evolution of Guelph's transit system is well illustrated, as is the coming of the automobile.

The square has periodically undergone rearrangement to suit the needs of the day. The most recent rationalization altered the road pattern through the square and closed one of the radiating streets. This was to make way for a new shopping centre—all part of a major urban renewal program which became necessary when shopping malls proliferated on the perimeter of the city.

Here, again, we see clear evidence that a city's finest architecture is a vulnerable target for those bent on mediocrity. Indeed, would "urban renewal" be necessary today if the best of the past had been protected and restored instead of demolished?

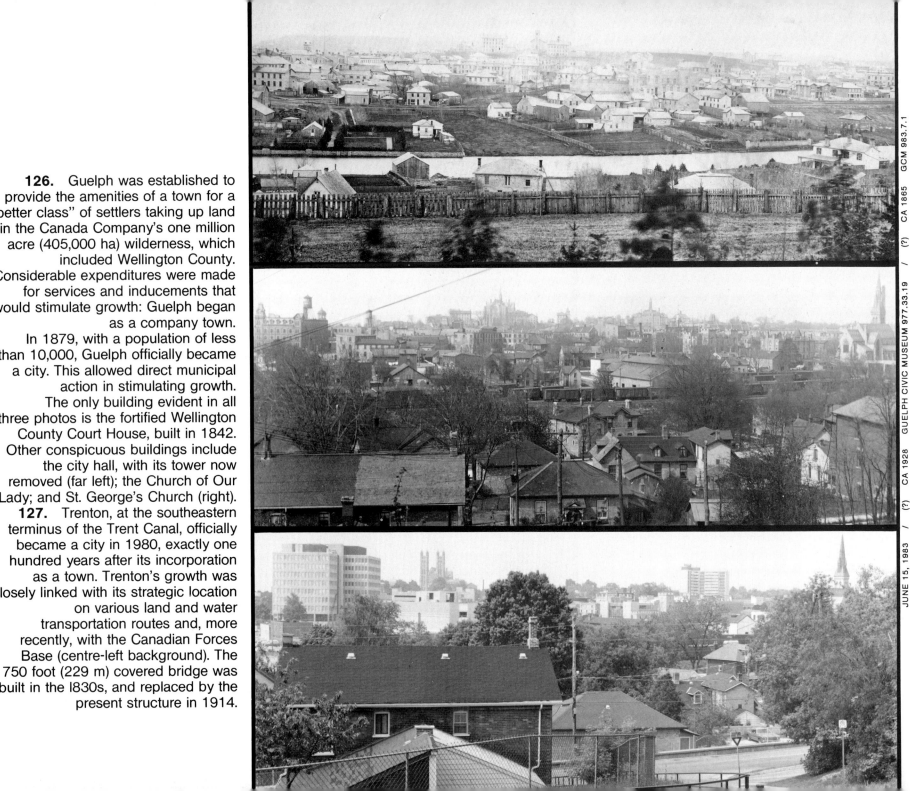

126. Guelph was established to provide the amenities of a town for a "better class" of settlers taking up land in the Canada Company's one million acre (405,000 ha) wilderness, which included Wellington County. Considerable expenditures were made for services and inducements that would stimulate growth: Guelph began as a company town.

In 1879, with a population of less than 10,000, Guelph officially became a city. This allowed direct municipal action in stimulating growth.

The only building evident in all three photos is the fortified Wellington County Court House, built in 1842. Other conspicuous buildings include the city hall, with its tower now removed (far left); the Church of Our Lady; and St. George's Church (right).

127. Trenton, at the southeastern terminus of the Trent Canal, officially became a city in 1980, exactly one hundred years after its incorporation as a town. Trenton's growth was closely linked with its strategic location on various land and water transportation routes and, more recently, with the Canadian Forces Base (centre-left background). The 750 foot (229 m) covered bridge was built in the l830s, and replaced by the present structure in 1914.

CA 1865   GCM 983.7.1

(?)

GUELPH CIVIC MUSEUM 977.33.19

CA 1928   (?)

JUNE 15, 1983

OCT 2, 1983 / HERINGTON CA 1905 MARY ANNE ROBERTS

FROM THE MOUNTAIN. TRENTON. ONT.

128. It seems incredible that only 21 years separate this pair of photos taken from Upper James Street, looking north across downtown Hamilton. The only truly modern building in the 1963 photo is the city hall—so prominent then, but nearly lost among today's high rises. Beyond, sailing on the harbour, are numerous pleasure craft; on the far shore, Burlington is barely visible through the haze.

129. Farther east along the escarpment, at Wentworth Street, an inclined railway operated from 1900 to 1936. Thereafter, wooden stairs scaled Hamilton Mountain, but now a four-lane road, angling up the escarpment, bisects the stairs. Although derelict, dangerous, and officially closed, the stairs are still in use. Meanwhile, trees have completely overgrown the old railway bed; this necessitated a slight change in the camera's point of view.

129

130. The view to the south on Eramosa Road displays two fine examples of Guelph's surviving stone architecture. In the late 1920s, the imposing towers of the Church of Our Lady were a very recent addition to the city's skyline. To the left, the Wellington Hotel was run-down after decades of various commercial uses. With the aid of the federal government, the building was restored and refurbished as an office building in the 1970s.

131. A few blocks west from downtown Peterborough, Charlotte Street passes through a five-way intersection. The awkward street layout left a small, odd-shaped lot, which is occupied by an asymmetrical building. Though hardly an architectural gem, it survives—a comment, perhaps, on its fitness to exploit this unusual niche. As a grocery store, in the days before cars were plentiful, its delivery trucks were well-known around the city. Today, as a corner variety, it is the customer's vehicles which come and go.

In Southern Ontario, it is in this part of a town or city—the part adjacent to downtown—that we are most likely to encounter the uncommon landscape where trees appear to be losing ground.

CA 1930 / (?) GUELPH CIVIC MUSEUM 977.33.3

JUNE 15, 1983

132

132. On Queen's Avenue, London, at Wellington Street, not far from downtown, the Forest City has lost some of its trees. But the apartment buildings thus exposed are well kept and visually interesting compared with the concrete box next door.

133. The homes on Aberdeen Street in Fort Erie were built in the early 1950s on what had been a farmer's field. By 1959, virtually all the trees in today's photo were already established.

I took the 1959 photo to the doors of several of these homes. At one of them I was greeted by a woman with a don't-sell-me-anything look. I explained what I was doing as she studied the photo intently. Suddenly a smile broke across her face; "Hey! Those are our kids there!"

134-5. Dufferin Avenue, Brantford, exemplifies the eclectic elegance of late Victorian housing. However, the house on the left has been completely renovated, which made it difficult to find. The outlined photo offers an approximate point of view, while the others show details of neighbouring houses. Notice how the trim, without exception, has gone from dark to light, a phenominon which is evident in many of the photo pairs in this book.

AUG 20, 1983

136. Palmerston Avenue, Toronto, as seen from Harbord Street, was very new when the 1908 photograph was taken. By the mid-1920s it had become a shaded, tree-lined street. Today, these trees have reached maturity, and the view will probable open up considerably over the next decade or two—until a new generation takes their place!

From this evidence, it seems reasonable to surmise that modern subdivisions can be expected to become similarly forested in time.

137ab. Like most Ontario roads in the horse and buggy era, Toronto's Danforth Avenue developed impassable mud holes in wet weather. In 1910, it was undoubtedly the photographer's purpose to draw attention to this situation. Roads quickly improved as the automobile became popular.

137cd. Looking east toward Yonge Street, St. Clair Avenue West has changed beyond recognition since 1910. Modern buildings have replaced stately pines, though side streets in the area remain well treed. The street is under construction as old streetcar tracks are being removed.

W. JAMES   CA 1915   CTA 485   /   APR 26, 1984

138. By 1900, a new building technology which utilized steel skeletons was permitting cities to grow vertically as never before. On Yonge Street at Wellington, one of Toronto's earliest "skyscrapers" was photographed in 1907 and is still extant.

139. Bay Street was completely rebuilt after the Great Toronto Fire of 1904, however, few of this generation of buildings can be found today. At the top of the street, the Old City Hall (1899) narrowly escaped both the fire and, in the early 1960s, the wrecker's ball.

140-1. Toronto Street has been aptly described as "the street that died." Perhaps the finest grouping of nineteenth-century commercial buildings on the continent was destroyed for the sake of a parking garage and a few modern office buildings, including the Revenue Canada monstrosity (bright green!) at the end of the street.

142. From the tower of the Canada Life Building, which was still under construction in 1929, there is a splendid view of University Avenue and the north-central area of the city. A few landmarks are visible in both photographs, including the Ontario Legislature. With each passing year, however, the view is being hemmed in by monolithic newcomers.

143ab. On the northeast corner of Yonge and Shuter, the primary function of an old clapboard building appears to be to provide a substrate for its splash of advertisements. Note how the "Empire Wallpaper Co." building was later extended to include the entire corner.

143cd. In 1926 on Queen Street east of York there was a block of buildings which dated from the days of "Muddy York." Here, too, we see a plethora of signs; this contrasts sharply with the sanitized, clean-cut appearance of the imposing Sheraton Centre.

144-5. Looking west on Front Street, the Gooderham Building has replaced the "Coffin Block" with an equally curious wedge. In this area, many old buildings have been given a new lease on life. But it is the $57 million CN Tower—the world's tallest freestanding structure—that dominates the scene.

CITY OF TORONTO ARCHIVES 10090   W. JAMES   1929   JULY 24, 1984

144

CHAPTER SEVEN

Industry

Hamilton's steel industries form one of the nation's most dramatic and familiar industrial landscapes. Just before sunrise, the fires and lights of night blend with the stark grey-black, haze-shrouded daytime reality. It is a scene in which form is derived entirely from function. And yet for most of us it is an enigmatic and vaguely terrifying spectacle. Nothing appears human in scale. It is as though this landscape exists for machinery's sake: steel-making machinery made by machines for the purpose of making steel for still more machines!

But this is industry at a high stage of development. In their infancy, processing and manufacturing in Southern Ontario were a direct outgrowth of the agricultural economy. Without the benefit of the wealth of Upper Canada's soils, industrialization would never have come about. Although the longstanding historical connection between farm and factory grows less apparent and less important with each passing decade, it remains vital for the majority of smaller rural communities, where a cheese factory, creamery, or feed mill may well be the single largest employer. And even our larger cities still maintain an important exchange between farm gate and factory door. The Toronto Stock Yards is a good example.

In the early days, a small cluster of farms often justified the erection of a grist mill—or a sawmill, still, blacksmith shop, or tannery. The simple machinery of these operations required nowhere near the amount of energy demanded by modern industries, but mills in particular needed more mechanical power than men or horses could supply. The waterwheel was, then, the only practical source of energy. Since there were many streams that could be readily harnessed and also because roads were very poor, mills sprang up every few miles throughout the settled regions.

As transportation improved, allowing access to wider markets, the capacity of successful mills was soon restricted by the amount of available waterpower. This limitation was exacerbated by the steadily increasing severity of spring floods and summer lows, problems which resulted from the clearing of forests and the draining of swamps in watersheds upstream. Bigger and better dams and the invention of the turbine provided some relief. Also, the invention of the steam engine provided an alternative, but these solutions were expensive, especially for the smaller mills. By the end of the nineteenth century, there existed a full-blown energy crisis.

Ultimately, the solution came from harnessing the vast, unused power of Niagara Falls and other large waterpower sites. Their energy was converted to electricity which could be sent almost anywhere. Many of the small waterpower sites continued to provide auxiliary power for a time, but by the 1950s very few remained in operation.

When energy production had to be combined with manufacturing facilities, it was usually the need for energy which determined the location. The steam engine had begun to lift this site constraint, but it took electricity to completely free plants to locate wherever they could best meet their needs for transportation facilities, cheap labour, or convenient waste disposal. Twentieth-century industrial expansion became more or less synonymous with the growth of cities.

Today, we speak of the "post-industrial era." But this is not to say that industry is fading away—it is as productive as ever. Rather, its paramount importance in the economy has been eclipsed by the service sector; e.g. information, communications, transportation, and entertainment. Office towers have replaced factories as the standard symbol of achievement. But factories and the landscapes of industry will always be with us. The challenge, in this new era, is to get a better grasp on their ability to shape our society and our environment.

Facing page: Steel mills, Hamilton, Nov. 18, 1984.

In order to harness the power of rivers, dams were built to increase the "head" and divert some or all of the flow through a waterwheel or turbine. The earliest dams often resembled beaver dams, but sooner or later these washed out in spring floods. Their replacements were invariably larger and more permanent.

148. On the North Thames River in the town of St. Marys, an impressive dam, built in 1907, holds back a small lake that has become as much a part of the landscape as the river itself. Like much of the town, the dam was built from local limestone. And like many old dams, this one has fallen into disrepair since it is no longer economically functional.

149. The Chats Falls Generating Station on the Ottawa River was built during the 1930s using steel-reinforced concrete. Such a large-scale project would have been impossible with nineteenth-century construction methods, and pointless, too, before long distance transmission of electricity had become a practical reality.

J. BOYD   JUNE 3, 1928   PAC PA-88041

J. BOYD   JUNE 17, 1923   PAC PA-86077

NOV 8, 1983

AUG 21, 1983

150

150ab. Of the many hundreds of small mills established in Ontario during the nineteenth century, only a few remain today. Wooden buildings, such as this one at Eldorado Park near Brampton, were particularly susceptible to fire, while other mills were simply abandoned and left to crumble.

150cd. At Norval (Halton R.M.), a larger mill has also disappeared, even though the brand-name flour produced here was highly acclaimed and was, for many years, a household staple throughout the region.

151. The Hayhoe Mill at Pine Grove (York R.M.) is a rare exception: it not only continues to operate, but has grown considerably. As a modern facility, it mills flour for the large bakeries. The roof of the original building can still be discerned among the numerous additions which now flank it. Once powered exclusively by a small branch of the Humber River, the use of this energy source was discontinued after a destructive flood in 1954.

152. In 1875, the flour mill in St. Jacobs (Waterloo R.M.) became the first in the country to replace mill stones with rollers. Waterpower was used here until just a few years before the mill closed in 1975. Supplementary steam power was also used until the arrival of "the hydro." Fire twice destroyed this mill, but it was tough competition which finally shut it down. The building and silos are now used, in an entirely different way, for shops and crafts. The rambling complex has dozens of nooks and crannies that invite exploration. In one corner the old turbine shaft is once again turning, providing power for the mill's lights. The waterpower system is now secure from neglect and decay that has destroyed most of Ontario's historic waterpower sites.

153. While grist mills and (temporary) sawmills were usually the first to be established, in many communities they were soon followed by other farm-related industries. In Galt (now Cambridge), a complex of woollen mills shared a race which flowed through the buildings. Today, instead of the usual total annihilation, "ruins" were deliberately left standing to form the basis of an interesting park.

154

As well as waterpower, inland rivers provided transportation in some locations. This was especially important in the pre-railway era, but remained significant right into this century.

154. The Thames is readily navigable from Lake St. Clair to Chatham, where the waterfront attracted a variety of industries. Prominent in this view is the Ward Mill. Today, the river is used only by pleasure craft, and the former industrial sites have become parkland.

155. Without dredging and damming, most rivers were too shallow to be of much use for moving freight. The Scugog River, flowing from Scugog Lake to Sturgeon Lake, was canalized in 1844 to the great benefit of Lindsay (Peterborough Co.). The traffic in wheat and lumber through this centre was a key factor in its rapid growth.

Recently, Public Works Canada has refurbished the dam and locks, which are now used solely for recreation. But fire has gutted the charming old mill and its future is uncertain.

156. Despite efforts to diversify Brantford's industrial base, the city remains heavily dependent on the manufacturing of farm machinery. On Market Street, not far from downtown, Massey Ferguson uses this remaining building as a warehouse.

157. Next door, no trace remains of another implement manufacturing plant. These industries originally located here to take advantage of the canal (in the foreground, and already defunct) which once carried freight to Lake Erie. Later this corridor was used by a railway. Now the area is undergoing redevelopment; plans include a telecommunications museum on the site of the former Cockshutt plant.

The architecture of these factories is typical of a bygone era. More than mere style, it reflects the technology of the day. Bricks form the outer walls, but inside nearly everything is wooden. Rows of heavy timbers support exposed joists and hardwood floors. The characteristic three-storey height was made practical by the use of elevators as well as stairs. Aided by the relative narrowness of these structures, numerous windows lit their interiors. Line shafts supplied power to the machinery, which also made it convenient to have long, narrow buildings.

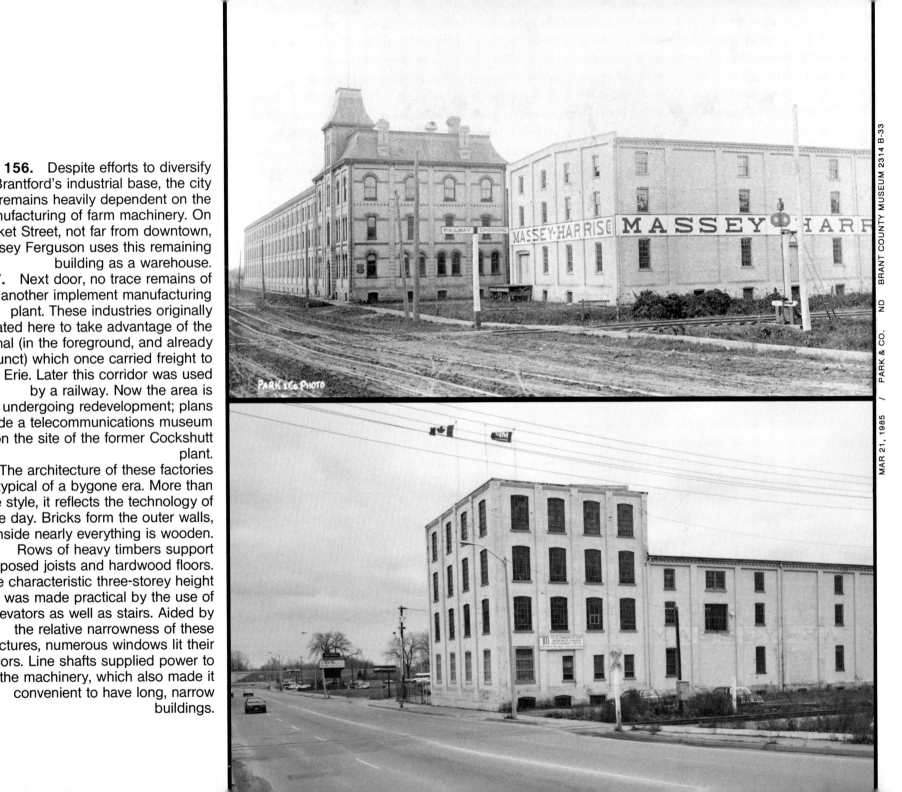

AUG 13, 1983   /   (?)   1924   PAC PA-31431

SEPT 22, 1983   /   (?)   1923   PAC PA-31074

158

SEPT 29, 1983 / MAGIE 1919

Old-fashioned factories are such commonplace elements in the landscape that we scarcely notice them. But they are rapidly being displaced by sprawling, modern plants in industrial parks, and they will, no doubt, eventually become scarce.

158ab. A Walkerton (Bruce Co.) furniture factory is still operational, though the business has seen many ups and downs. Furniture sales are particularly susceptible to the general state of the economy.

158cd. Peas, corn, apples, pork and beans, chickens, and even ducks were processed at the Dominion Canners plant in Strathroy (Middlesex Co.). During its peak years in the early 1900s, many tons of canned goods were exported annually. Today, the building is used mainly for warehousing.

159. In Peterborough, this once prosperous foundry is remembered only by older residents. The sign on the far end of the buildings reads: "SAWMILL & PULP MILL MACHINERY, WATERWHEELS." Only the building on the left remains.

160-1. These aerial views show the dramatic growth of Hamilton's steel industries. Hemmed in, the industrial area has expanded out into the harbour on an artificial landfill. In some places the water's edge has been moved nearly one mile (1.5 km) from the natural shoreline.

159

SEPT 5, 1985

161

162. It was not the discovery of crude oil, but rather a method for making something useful (kerosene) from it that led to the digging (by hand!) of North America's first commercial oil well at Oil Springs (Lambton Co.) in 1858. There was so much oil here that many "gushers" spewed it out faster than it could be put into barrels. Oil Springs rapidly became a wild boom town. Many service industries, such as the twelve general stores, nine hotels, and the daily newspaper, were short-lived. But a trickle of "black gold" is still produced here today, and this old machine shop still maintains the machinery of the oil patch.

163. In the early days there were twenty small refineries at Oil Springs and fifty-two at London. Through consolidation Imperial Oil was born and the refining operations moved to Sarnia to take advantage of cheap water transportation.

The Imperial Oil Refinery of 1923 was inefficient, wasteful, foul-smelling and dangerous by modern standards. Not only are today's operations getting cleaner, but efforts are also being made to soften the edges of the high-tech landscape with lawns, flowers, and trees. Change is continual here; the point of view was selected by analogy alone.

163

CHAPTER EIGHT

Transportation

IF A DOZEN darts were randomly thrown at a wall map of Southern Ontario, and we then travelled to the points indicated by the pinholes— What kinds of places would we find? How far, on average, would we be from the nearest road?

Ignoring the darts that fell on lakes, we would almost certainly find ourselves in a dense forest at some point, many hard miles of hiking from the nearest road. And we would likely hit a corn field, where it might only seem like a long way from a road. But chances are that we would not hit a roadway, though we might come close sometimes.

And yet, just over half the photos in this book represent "direct hits." That is, they were taken by photographers who stood on roads or sidewalks. Of the rest, more than half depict a road somewhere in the view. Clearly, then, this collection of photos does not represent randomly selected locations. It is only natural that we see the landscape from the pathways we frequent, but how often are we conscious of this bias in our viewpoint?

In the days when dark forests shrouded the landscape, rivers and lakes opened the way to the new settlements. These waterways offered luxurious travelling compared with the quagmires, pitch-holes, sideling slopes, stumps, rocks, fords, and corduroy roads that the inland traveller faced. No wonder the settlers took such a dim view of the forest and saw it only as a hindrance to progress.

Nor is it any wonder that the railways seemed so marvelous. From the speed and comfort of the train, coach windows offered a whole new way of looking at the landscape. Like theatre patrons, passengers gazed with detachment at fields and farms that flickered by in an endless, moving panorama.

The iron horse made tracks through the landscape, but it barely participated in it. The horseless carriage, on the other hand, almost from the moment it first spluttered onto the scene, began to interact with the landscape. Whereas railways were confined to long, narrow lines across the landscape, the auto followed almost everywhere the horse had been. Mud became gravel, then pavement; fences transformed into curbs, guard rails, and noise barriers; pastures were replaced by parking lots; and stables gave way to garages.

In the Automobile Age, cars have become extensions of our homes— comfortable moving verandahs from which we can safely survey our world. In fact, most of what we know about the landscape is what we gather through our car windows. But we have a tendency to look straight ahead. And the faster we go, the more forceful this instinct becomes. Quite unlike rail passengers, motorists set their own schedule and may alter their course at the slightest whim. Therefore, the roadside landscape is often deliberately and dramatically oriented toward catching the peripheral vision of the motorist. The familiar roadscape of service stations, motels, and fast food outlets—the strip—is garish and trendy. For the pedestrian, it is downright inhospitable. Huge signs, bright lights, bold contrasts and colours, and gaudy architecture are all designed to grab our attention. The strip is an extreme case in that it is *so* intentional. But every inhabited roadside landscape has some of this tendency to display toward the road. Even an uninhabited woodlot has its hydro line and its roadside refuse.

Nothing captures the exhilaration of the approaching dawn of the twenty-first century quite like a fast tour on a downtown expressway, especially at night when the traffic eases and the whole city seems to drift by in a phantom of lights. Perhaps in the future some personalized flying machine will displace the car as the common method of travel. Until then, the landscape will continue to wear its many faces to the road.

Facing page: Highway 401, Weston (Metro Toronto), Apr. 26, 1984.

(?)   1905   PUBLIC ARCHIVES CANADA C-23187   /   JUNE 24, 1983

166. The Rideau Canal, completed in 1832, was built to provide a safe route for military traffic between Montreal and Kingston. The St. Lawrence route was regarded as being too vulnerable in the event of renewed American aggression. Between Bytown (Ottawa) and Kingston, forty-seven locks were required to overcome a 280 foot (85 m) height of land.

At the southern end of the Rideau Lakes, Jones Falls was the site of a long series of locks. A dam built here was the second highest and perhaps the most impressive in the world at the time—a stone wall holding back 60 feet (18 m) of water. From near the top of this dam, our view from a back yard would have been shut out long ago except for the owner's judicious cutting of the trees.

167. Where the Rideau Canal meets the Ottawa River, rough-and-tumble Bytown grew up, becoming the City of Ottawa in 1854 and the capital of Canada four years later. The Ottawa River had been a major highway for the fur trade for two centuries, and it became equally important for the exploitation of central Canada's vast pine forests. Here we see the end of that era; this is the last of the great lumber rafts on its way to Quebec, slipping past the Supreme Court and the House of Commons.

167

168. The Trent Canal System, following an ancient canoe route, required only 33 miles (53km) of man-made channels to complete a 240 mile (384km) water course. Begun in 1833 on a small scale on the Kawartha Lakes, the system was not completed until 1920. Commercial traffic declined as roads improved, but recreational use soon began taking up the slack, as we see here at Fenelon Falls.

169. It is not quite accurate to say that the Trent Canal was completed: the Holland River Division was never finished. In a bizarre attempt at pork barrelling, the government began a canal to connect the faithful Liberal stronghold of Newmarket with Lake Simcoe. Dredging and the building of three locks was nearing completion and over half a million dollars had been spent when the Conservatives won the election of 1911. They immediately put a halt to the work. Today, the three locks remain almost exactly as they were when abandoned. Too large and durable to be forgotten or ignored, the stoneworks stand as rather picturesque monuments to patronage and stupidity.

J. BOYD   AUG 15, 1923   PAC PA-86269

JULY 9, 1983

169

170. National security worries aside, the St. Lawrence River route was obviously worthy of canalization. But work on bypassing the many difficult rapids was carried out in piecemeal fashion; it was not until 1848 that a viable steamer route was opened between Montreal and Lake Ontario.

The old Cornwall Canal can be seen at the bottom of the photo of the Long Sault Rapids. This all disappeared under Lake St. Lawrence, part of the Seaway development which was undertaken jointly by Canada and the United States in the 1950s.

171. At Port Colborne, the southern entrance to the Welland Canal was photographed from a raised lift bridge which is still operating today. In 1929, the canal was still under construction, with dredging in progress in the foreground. While 1932 marked the opening of the modern phase of the canal, its history goes back to 1824 when a Canadian entrepreneur formed a private company to build and operate the first tiny canal to bypass Niagara Falls. Construction and maintenance costs were unprofitably high, but the utility of the Welland Canal was unquestionably demonstrated by the time the government became involved in 1841.

171

Where roads and railways crossed rivers or canals, extraordinary engineering was often required. Railway bridges in particular have been one of the most frequently photographed elements in the landscape. Perhaps it is their symbolism—technology rising above nature—which explains their photogenic appeal.

172. At the west end of Burlington Bay, the Desjardins Canal helped make the town of Dundas more prominent than Hamilton in the days before the railways. The double track carries rail traffic between Toronto and Hamilton, across the abandoned canal.

173. The entrance to Burlington Bay was blocked by a sand spit until a channel was opened through it in 1832. In 1952, a freighter rammed the lift bridge in the older photo; its replacement dwarfs the old lighthouse. But even this bridge was eclipsed by the Burlington Skyway (partially visible on the left) which was completed in 1958.

The coming of railways in the 1850s took the wind out of the canal builders' sails. Public enthusiasm shifted to the new technology; railways would, at last, make Canada truly prosperous. In a mad scramble to lay track, duplication, waste and scandal were the order of the day. Few railways ever paid a satisfactory return to their investors. And although the country as a whole did benefit, it was not to the extent predicted by early proponents.

174. The Kingston and Pembroke Railway was built in the 1880s through some very difficult country. The photos show a causeway that crosses Calabogie Lake. The area served by the line did not have the resources to keep it alive; this northern section was abandoned in the early 1960s.

175. The Credit Valley Railway was an ambitious, multi-branched line which ambled across Southern Ontario. It is at its scenic best here at the Forks of the Credit where it ascends the Niagara Escarpment. This line was opened in 1879; just four years later the C.V.R. was absorbed by Canadian Pacific. The station was closed in 1932, and passenger service discontinued in 1970.

The cliffs show scars where building stone for Ontario's Legislature was removed; the railway, of course, provided the transportation.

Until the turn of the century, railways detracted from the improvement of Ontario's abysmal roads. Except for the short-lived plank roads, even the best "highways" were at times impassable; lesser roads in the early years had many stumps and potholes which frequently caused horse-drawn vehicles to upset. Although roads were invariably opened in conjunction with settlement, substantial improvements to these muddy tracks came only with the appearance of the automobile.

176. Between Toronto and Hamilton, General Simcoe's Dundas Street, now Highway 5, became one of the first asphalt roads in the country in 1917. Seven years later, the cut through the escarpment near Burlington still looked like an open wound. But time has healed the landscape and the cut is hardly noticed by today's motorist.

177. Hugging the St. Lawrence between Kingston and Montreal, this dusty track was a major road, already a century old when the photograph was taken in 1893. Since the completion of the 401, Highway 2 carries mostly local traffic. At Johnstown, just east of Prescott, the highway crosses a small creek; in the distance, the Eisenhower Bridge spans the highway and the St. Lawrence.

177

178. Thousands of travellers cross this bridge on Highway 401 every day. But how many would recognize the scene?

Lock No. 2 of the Trent Canal is on the right, while at the other end of the control dam a small hydro-electric plant utilizes the drop in the Trent River.

179. This series of photos illustrates a typical succession of bridges on a secondary road: wooden, early concrete, and modern concrete. The second photo also hints at a ford on the extreme left, perhaps used during construction.

As the road has improved, the bridge and the creek have become almost invisible to the passing motorist. Note, too, how the the view has been restricted by the very considerable growth of trees.

In the background, Brantford's famous Mohawk Chapel, built in 1783, is the oldest Anglican church in Ontario. It has been visited twice by Queen Elizabeth II.

In former times bridges were a source of civic pride; even little ones were shrines to progress and civility. This is hardly surprising, given that most were built by local people, using local materials and know-how. In many instances, however, the earliest bridges were little better than early roads.

180. A caption on this photo reads: "The Bridge, Westwood" (Peterborough Co.). It was built in 1893, using a steel panel-truss design which was then a novelty in rural areas. The old ford is still visible today. Note also the incandescent street light, a type seldom seen today though still common twenty years ago.

181. Gow's Bridge in Guelph is one of only half a dozen remaining stone-arch bridges in the province. The single-lane bridge is carefully maintained but the tannery, seemingly built to match, has unfortunately been lost.

182-3. A pastoral scene a few miles north of Marmora (Hastings Co.) has lost its charm. The straightened road now cuts through the granite hills; there are no sheep, not even in the fields; hydro pylons have displaced the rail fences; and the old barn disintegrates, while across the road a new house looks just like a thousand others.

AUG 1, 1983 / (?) / CA 1900 PAC C-27561

JULY 9, 1983

J. C. SMITH   CA 1900   B. (JIM) SMITH

A. E. DUFF   CA 1902   PAC D. H. LOWRY COLL. C-80013

SEPT 1, 1983

JUNE 26, 1983

184ab. Scane Sideroad, west of Ridgetown, is a typical township road. It has been built up and widened considerably, but the improvements have not included the replacement of the old, shady maple.

184cd. Looking east toward the hamlet of Blacks Corners (Lanark Co.), today's view retains only the roadside cedars. Most of the buildings are still there, but are now hidden by trees. A number of new houses have been built along the road in the past decade.

185. Early in 1796, Yonge Street from York to Lake Simcoe was "completed" in only four months! This thirty mile stretch has been one of the province's busiest roads ever since. At Newmarket we see a succession of improvements. In April of 1921, the road was a deeply rutted obstacle course; by September of that year it had been properly macadamized. But this was just one step in many toward today's four to six lanes of pavement.

The automobile brought with it a host of new scenes ranging from the car lot to the wrecking yard. But perhaps its most ubiquitous addition to the landscape has been the service station.

186. The Duffus Garage capitalized on the phenomenon from its beginning; by the early 1930s it had grown, diversified, and added considerable polish to its premises. For several decades it was one of Peterborough's leading car dealerships. In 1983, as a restaurant, the building retains few traces of its former use.

187. The intersection of Highways 86 and 23 has been the site of a service station for many years, and it would probably take as many photographs to tell the complete story of its evolution. The face of a service station is a sign of the times; it doesn't take very long for it to look dated. Even while preparing to take this picture there was a change: the price of gasoline suddenly dropped by ten cents per litre!

CHAPTER NINE

Special Places

THE PHOTOGRAPHS in Chapter One portrayed some of the physiographic aspects of Southern Ontario's landscapes, while subsequent chapters dealt with some major ways in which human hands have modified the landscape. There remains, however, a collection of odds and ends—gardens, beaches, waterfalls, parks, monuments, and a variety of public buildings. This diversity might seem too great even for a catch-all chapter, but there is a shared element. These landscapes are not incidental byproducts of whatever human endeavours, but rather, they have been deliberately preserved, manipulated, or created for their own sake. They are not ordinary landscapes, though in some instances their familiarity or fame may belie their uniqueness.

Sometime in the remote past, Man's intentional manipulation of the landscape must have begun with gardening. It remains one of our most intimate involvements with landscapes. Gardens rectify the deficiencies of a less-than-perfect world.

The transition from gardens to parks seems like a small step, but, in fact, *public* parks are a comparatively recent idea. A park is both a playground and a Nature preserve. As a playground, it may facilitate hunting, fishing, observing Nature, camping, travelling, or mere contented idleness. These are primeval activities stemming from deep motivations, from subconscious links with our prehistoric roots. No wonder they are pursued with such intensity and rewarded with such profound satisfaction. Modern times have witnessed a steady erosion of possibilities for these pursuits; hence, the need for parks of all kinds is constantly increasing. As a preserve, a park is commonly thought of as a vast tract of relatively undisturbed wilderness, but a symbolic grove of trees, in the form of a city park, serves a similar purpose.

From the sculptured leisure of the city park, we cross the street to consider the more formal landscape of religion. A church is in many respects the opposite of a factory. Spiritual rather than material concerns shape a church: a religious edifice is steeped in symbolism, tradition, and history rather than modern technology. Traditionally, wood and stone or brick are used to express abiding faith. On a symbolic level, churches can be compared with city parks, which are representative of Nature, and with monuments, which immortalize our heroes.

Other types of public buildings—rural schools, railway stations, and libraries—are also illustrated in this chapter. To a degree they are like churches in that their architecture is intended to inspire awe and humility. Their designs clearly show more utilitarian influences, but they too reflect a striving toward symbolic importance and monolithic permanence. Nowhere is this more evident, or more appropriate, than on Parliament Hill, where our sense of history and national identity is enshrined in distinctly un-American fashion.

Public buildings and public parks, though by no means immune from the wrecking ball and bulldozer, on the whole show greater stability and permanence than most other cultural features of the landscape. Given our climate of continual change, it seems likely that their place in the landscape will grow still more prominent. And as their perceived value increases, perhaps their future grows more secure.

Wide recognition and respect for landmarks and special places should have a stabilizing effect on both society and its landscapes. It is interesting to note that many of the photos in this chapter are of places where Ontario's adolescent landscapes are beginning to take on a degree of maturity. Although in this respect they cannot rival the common landscapes of the Old World, most of these places have mellowed considerably and many appear to have achieved some ecological stablity.

Facing page: Lake Doré, Renfrew Co., June 26, 1983.

190. The Maitland Golf Club in Goderich is seen here in a 1924 photograph. The growth of shrubs and trees has softened this landscape considerably, but the effect has been offset by the stark architecture of the Club's new building.

191. Of the hundreds of landscapes investigated in the preparation of this book, Witt's Garden in Pembroke has the dubious distinction of having fared the worst. This beautifully landscaped scene was cultivated by a hobbyist (a retired doctor it is thought), but little else is known. The garden has been virtually forgotten; even its location could be determined only by an intensive field search. (The white house at the centre of the photo proved to be the key.) The history of the garden and its conversion to a landfill and snow dump site remains obscure.

192-3. Just the opposite has happened at Hamilton's west entrance: a gravel pit has been transformed into a beautiful garden. The Rock Garden is the centrepiece of a network of woodland, parks, and waterways known collectively as the Royal Botanical Gardens. Although only one year old in 1931, much had already been accomplished; Nature's work, however, was just beginning.

194. Stratford's formal Shakespearean garden was developed on the site of a burned-out factory. The ruins were cleared away except for the chimney which became a focal point. On the south bank of the Avon River, within easy walking distance of the Festival Theatre, the garden features a bust of the old bard himself. In recent years the trees and shrubs have grown up considerably, depriving the garden of some of its formality. In the background, the Perth County Courthouse is one of the city's prominent landmarks.

195. Looking upstream from almost the same location, a small dam holds back a rather extensive lake. Although built for pragmatic reasons, the waterpower potential was too small to be of lasting significance. The lake, however, was soon recognized as an aesthetic asset, and it became an integral part of Stratford's landscape. Work on the watercourse gradually produced a scene that appears more civilized, and yet more natural. Today's view (not shown) is foreshortened by still more trees on the river bank. The evolution of this place typifies a general trend in the landscape, and illustrates a changing attitude toward the environment. Exploitation is slowly giving way to stewardship, though we still have a very long way to go.

SEPT 3, 1983 / (?) CA 1925 PAC PA-31792

OCT 3, 1983 / 1913 PAC PA-10587 W. J. TOPLEY

196ab.   Springbank Park in London is best known for its "Storybook Gardens," a children's fantasy land. The park stretches along the south bank of the Thames, on the city's west side. The trees here have been entirely replaced by a new generation, while the flower beds and stone steps have given way to the less labour-intensive lawn.

196cd.   A few miles from Belleville, across the Bay of Quinte, Massassauga Park was a favourite destination for excursionists of the pork-pie hat and picnic basket era. The park, not readily accessible by car even today, gradually declined in popularity.

The incredibly slow growth of the old red cedar on the right is worth noting. In seventy years it hardly seems to have grown an inch, although its progeny have established themselves on the lawn nearby and are probably growing much more rapidly.

197.   Returning once again to Stratford, upstream from the dam in the previous photos, the lake lies mirror-still on an October morning in 1930. A June afternoon can hardly match the serenity of the older view, and yet it is evident that the potential is still here.

197

198. Waterfalls often form the central feature of parks; even an artificial fall, as we see here at Belfountain (Peel R. M.), has its appeal. This park began as a private effort, but it has since been taken over by the Credit Valley Conservation Authority. As the park's popularity keeps growing, an admission fee helps to keep limits on the number of users. The fountain topped with a bell is carefully maintained, but unfortunately the fountains built into the retaining wall have become clogged with lime over the years.

199. Eugenia Falls, at the head of the Beaver Valley (Grey Co.) was once an impressive cascade. Since 1915, all but a trickle has been diverted through a hydro-electric plant. The area around the falls is now preserved as a park.

200-1. The Tooth of Time, perched precariously at the head of the Elora Gorge (Wellington Co.), has been the subject of legends, poems, paintings, and countless photographs. The village of Elora owes its beginnings to the waterpower potential here on the Grand River. Industry is still active on the river banks, though only tourism now benefits directly from the waterfall. Concrete repairs protect the "Tooth" from further erosion.

AUG 21, 1983 / J. BOYD JUNE 23, 1918 PAC PA-71075

(?) ND GREY COUNTY MUSEUM 979.53.22 / SEPT 11, 1983

201

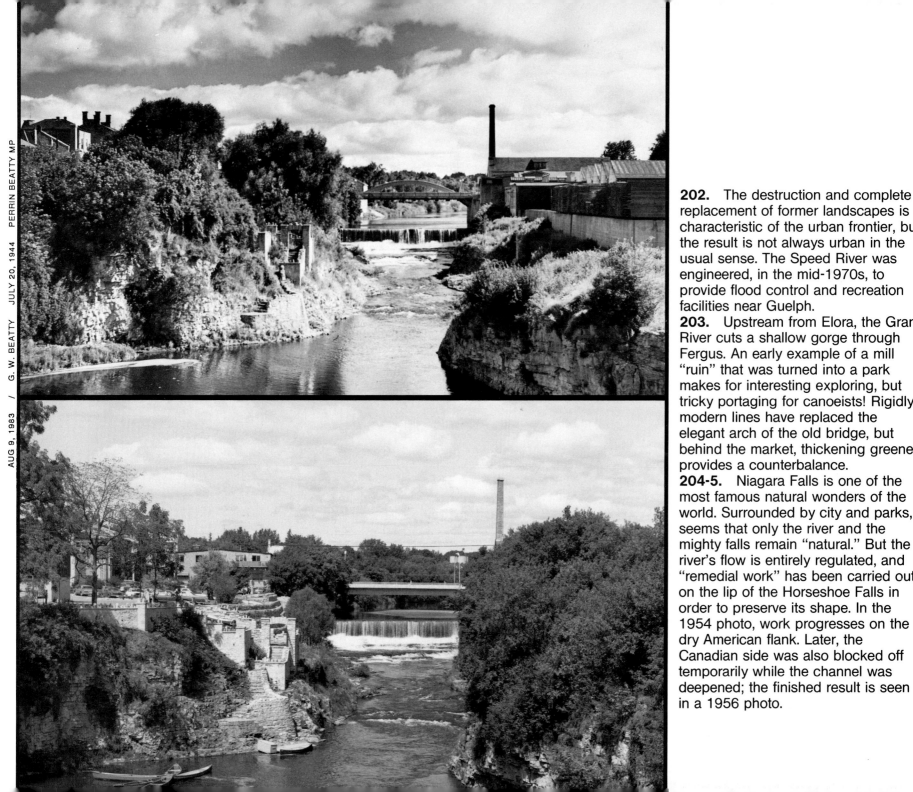

202. The destruction and complete replacement of former landscapes is characteristic of the urban frontier, but the result is not always urban in the usual sense. The Speed River was engineered, in the mid-1970s, to provide flood control and recreation facilities near Guelph.

203. Upstream from Elora, the Grand River cuts a shallow gorge through Fergus. An early example of a mill "ruin" that was turned into a park makes for interesting exploring, but tricky portaging for canoeists! Rigidly modern lines have replaced the elegant arch of the old bridge, but behind the market, thickening greenery provides a counterbalance.

204-5. Niagara Falls is one of the most famous natural wonders of the world. Surrounded by city and parks, it seems that only the river and the mighty falls remain "natural." But the river's flow is entirely regulated, and "remedial work" has been carried out on the lip of the Horseshoe Falls in order to preserve its shape. In the 1954 photo, work progresses on the dry American flank. Later, the Canadian side was also blocked off temporarily while the channel was deepened; the finished result is seen in a 1956 photo.

206. Special places, such as this beach at Point Pelee, sometimes require special measures to preserve them from the wear and tear of the crowds they attract. The southernmost tip of mainland Canada became a National Park in 1918. Today, it is one of our smallest National Parks and also one of the most heavily used. The park's popularity endangered the unique and fragile ecology of "the tip." This 1968 photo makes it evident that something had to be done. The solution, implemented in 1971, was a propane-powered transit system which takes visitors on a free ten-minute ride to the end of the road. From there it is a short walk to the end of land. The perspective was slightly altered, but the clump of cedars on the right helps to identify the location.

207. Wasaga Beach, at the southern end of Georgian Bay, is much more extensive than Pelee's narrow tip. But here too it makes sense to restrict cars. The beach may no longer be used as a roadway as it was in the 1930s. Far removed from its natural state, this stretch of sandy beach and dunes has become a highly commercialized playground.

SEPT 2, 1983 / (?) / JULY 8, 1968 POINT PELEE NATIONAL PARK B661

PLAYLAND PARK
GAMES ARCADE RIDES

208. Looking back toward the previous point of view at Wasaga Beach, we can see two false fronts—one rectangular, and the other with a distinctive curved top. These provided the only definite clue as to the exact location of the photos. But even these buildings have been moved from their original positions; high water and occasional storms forced a general retreat. The large hotel and some other buildings were destroyed by fire. Others were demolished; most are remembered only by long-time residents.

209. While sandy beaches are undoubtedly the most popular, rocky beaches and limestone cliffs, in fact all types of waterfront lots, command premium prices. Whippoorwill Bay, near Lions Head (Bruce Co.), offers some of the finest cottage settings anywhere on the Great Lakes. The water here is deep and cold—too cold for comfortable swimming—but so clean you can drink it!

Unfortunately, there is hardly enough Great Lakes shoreline to meet the demand, and developers are putting tremendous pressure on our few remaining natural lakeshore environments. We urgently need places like the Bruce Peninsula National Park to protect our long-term interests.

209

210. A public square in the centre of town was in many instances the first park in a community. Churches often located either in the middle of the square or on its periphery. The connection was more than a casual one, however, because Sunday was not only a day of worship but also a day of leisure—an opportunity to enjoy a park.

In Cambridge (formerly Galt), churches dominate the square; this is the Knox Presbyterian, built in 1889. The height of the spire is, perhaps, a good indication of the wealth of the faithful at the time of construction. Next door was an opera house—a mark of social refinement once considered *de rigueur* in any self-respecting town or city.

211ab. At Rockton (Hamilton-Wentworth R. M.), the Anglican church is used irregularly and the yard shows signs of decline—leaning gravestones and old, sagging fences—though the building is in good repair.

211cd. Across the province, hundreds of small rural churches are bravely maintained, but many suffer from declining attendance and increasing costs. Many are Anglican, relics of a failed attempt to establish a state church in Upper Canada. St. Peter's Anglican, near Tyrconnell (Elgin Co.), is a typical white frame edifice. Buried in the cemetery nearby is Col. Thomas Talbot, who figured so prominently in the region's settlement.

Appendix

SOME OF THE more technical aspects of the rephotography process are summarized in this appendix. It is intended to provide practical information and advice for those who may be interested in exploring this branch of photography.

Equipment. Ideally, the same equipment used to make an original photograph should be used to make the new photo. Unfortunately, this is rarely possible or practical.

Photographers of yesterday had to work much harder than their modern counterparts. Their equipment was cumbersome at best; their films—earlier, their wet glass plates—and lenses were much slower. But despite these handicaps, they often produced photographs of outstanding quality. In many cases, the quality cannot easily be equalled even with the best modern small- and medium-format equipment. Only unwieldy sheet-film cameras, normally used in the studio, can compare favourably.

My initial choice of a camera was a twin-lens reflex roll-film model with a sharp 75 mm lens. I reasoned that this film size would provide fine-grained negatives without the expense and awkwardness of sheet film. I soon discovered, however, that the angle-of-view of the noninterchangeable lens was not as wide as required to match many of the photos. Landscape photographers of old, it seems, preferred wide-angle lenses, and sometimes used very wide lenses. I therefore purchased a second roll-film camera, this time with interchangeable (65 and 100 mm) lenses and film backs (6x7 and 6x9 cm). From then on, I used the 65 mm lens almost exclusively, cropping the negatives as needed.

Another problem encountered was that of duplicating the swings and tilts used to control the convergence of verticals in some architectural photographs. Since these adjustments were not available to me, I thought I would not be able to match this aspect of the original photography.

Eventually, though not in time to prevent some mistakes, I learned that this need not be a problem. It is only necessary to keep the camera centred on the horizon (level) in order to prevent the unwanted convergence of verticals. Excess foreground was then cropped away in printing. It is important to note, however, that this simple technique requires a sufficiently wide lens. By the same token, any convergence in an original photograph can be matched by applying just the right amount of vertical inclination to the camera.

Any 35 mm SLR camera can be used for rephotography. The smaller format may produce more graininess that is apparent in most old originals, but this can be minimized by using slow film and a fine-grain developer.

A good selection of wide-angle lenses will minimize the need for cropping—28, 35, and 50 mm should cover most photographs likely to be encountered. Good modern zoom lenses nearly match prime lenses in overall performance, however, there are few zooms on the market with focal lengths of less than 35 mm. For certain occasions, a super-wide lens in the 17 to 21 mm range maybe useful.

Every lens design is unique with respect to the amount of radial distortion inherent in the image it produces. But since the amount of distortion is small and seldom apparent, it should be of little concern. It may be worth noting, however, that modern prime lenses suffer less from this defect than older lenses. Zoom lenses, on the other hand, commonly show considerable barrel distortion and may provide a better match for old wide-angle lenses.

Wherever possible, a tripod and cable release should be used, especially with slow films. With a tripod, there is no need to sacrifice depth of field in order to get a needle sharp picture. Special circumstances, such as those

Facing page: A perspective on architectural heritage, Toronto, Aug. 25, 1986.

encountered when rephotographing waterfalls, may sometimes require the use of a time exposure of several seconds. A neutral density filter with a factor of about 10X should be used to prevent gross over-exposure.

The frustration of finding blocked or unattainable points of view eventually led me to develop a "pole-pod." It consists of six and nine foot (2 and 3 m) lengths of one inch (25 mm) aluminum pipe which can be used separately or threaded together. On the top of the pole, a ball-and-socket tripod head is used to hold a 35 mm camera. I used a 20 mm lens with this rig since framing the photo requires some guesswork. The built-in timer or a remote release cam be used to trigger the shutter. Photos on pages 35, 102, and 125 were made with the aid of this device, and I would have used it more often if I had always had it with me.

A simple but absolutely essential piece of equipment is a clipboard to hold photocopies or dispensable copy prints for your field work. (*Never take an original into the field*. The slightest breeze or mishap could damage it and direct sunlight is hard on prints.) On many occasions I made copies of originals with a Polaroid Land camera fitted with a close-up lens. The quality was rather poor, but good enough for my purposes.

A copy of the original is essential. No matter how good your memory or how well you may know a picture, you will be wasting your time without some kind of copy with you in the field.

Perspective. A clear understanding of the difference between "perspective" and "field of view" (not to be confused with "depth of field") is essential in order to successfully rephotograph landscapes. Perspective refers to the *apparent* relationship of the objects that comprise the subject as seen from a given point of view. Perspective depends entirely on the choice of point of view; it is *not* a function of the focal length of a lens. Focal length and the size of the film format combine to determine field of view, i.e., how much the camera sees.

In other words, a photographer chooses a desired perspective by choosing a particular camera position (point of view), and then selects an appropriate lens to include the desired field of view. Thus, it is incorrect to speak of a "wide-angle perspective" or a "telephoto perspective." It is only the fields of view which differ. Of course, if a subject (a house for example) is photographed from a great distance with a telephoto lens it will look different than if the same subject were taken from the same direction but at close range with a wide-angle lens. But this is due to the photographer's change of position (and therefore also perspective) rather than differences inherent in the lens. The telephoto shot will include less background, and distance will appear compressed.

Near Waterloo (see text for explanation).

In the example opposite, a scene was photographed from a single point of view with a 35 mm wide-angle (top) and a 300 mm telephoto (bottom) on 35 mm film. The centre photo was made from a small portion of the same negative used for the top photo. Though quality has suffered due to extreme enlargement, the perspective is exactly the same.

The importance of all this to the rephotographic process is simple. It is essential that the precise camera *position*, in all three dimensions, be relocated in order to accurately duplicate the original perspective. The exact focal length of the lens is unimportant, provided that it is wide enough to include the entire field of the original.

Finding the Correct Perspective. Patience and attention to minute detail are the keys to relocating a specific point of view. As described in the Introduction, the technique basically involves relating various elements in the foreground to those in the background. Exploring the area covered by the photo will often reveal details which are no longer visible from the camera station. Usable elements are often very limited, or not particularly helpful—a hill for example—and the search for the correct perspective may be reduced to guesswork. In such cases I try to be doubly sure that the *location* is in fact the right one!

Having found an approximate point of view, move a few steps to either side and note how this changes the perspective. Use your eyes rather than the camera viewfinder. It is surprising how readily the relationship of the various elements can be changed. Having established the primary angle, move forward and backward along this imaginary line. This will produce more subtle changes in perspective, and finding the correct position in this dimension is more difficult. Finally, although photographs are usually made from eye-level, the vertical position of the camera must also be considered. Sometimes a photographer may have used a knoll, rock, or rooftop to gain elevation. Has the terrain under foot been altered since the original was made? If it has, it can be very disconcerting, and it can make accurate rephotography difficult or impossible.

If in doubt about the precise point of view, retake the photograph from several perspectives—but be systematic and take notes as you go. Later, in the darkroom, you can select the best shot after making a few trial prints. If it is convenient to return to the location, leave some kind of esoteric mark on the ground—often, available litter serves the purpose very well. You can then relocate the exact perspective of your earlier efforts, and make the necessary corrections.

Timing, Shadows, and Weather. The timing of a photograph can have a considerable bearing on its appearance. (For an extreme example,

compare the frontispiece with page 240.) Even a June photo will look somewhat different than a September shot, though this may concern only the purist. The difference is partly due to changes in vegetation, especially crops, and partly to changing shadows.

The length and position of shadows is also related to the time of day. Sometimes a bridge, building, or cliff may provide, by chance, a remarkably precise sundial (a typical example appears on page 172.)

Conversely, shadows can be useful in identifying a photographed location, especially if the date is known. On a given date and latitude, shadows will reach the length in the photo only twice during that day (or once at high noon). The corresponding horizontal sun angle (azimuth) is therefore reduced to one or two possibilities. From these, the camera's azimuth can be approximately deduced. If considerations such as the prevailing road-grid orientation are incorporated, no precise measurements or calculations are needed to produce useful results. (Both this subject and that of perspective can be more fully developed by applying mathematics as expounded in photogrammetry texts.)

Even when the date is unknown, most of the methods described above can still be applied, though with reduced precision. Shadows are always helpful since in north temperate latitudes they generally fall northward.

Cloudy or overcast conditions may be evident in a landscape photo only by the absence of shadows. For best results, such conditions should be matched at least in a general way. The same can be said of partial cloud cover or haze, though the effort may prove to be very demanding of time and patience.

In The Darkroom. In order to derive a satisfactory end product from your rephotographic efforts it is essential to have access to a darkroom. Your prints should match the original in size and cropping. This is easily achieved by putting the original or a same-size copy into the printing easel and setting the blades to match the original print size. Project your new negative onto the original, moving the enlarger up or down for best fit. (The visual effect of the combined images is very interesting!) Double check the focus and make a print to match the density and contrast of the original. The result should be an interesting pair of photographs— probably the closest thing to a time-travel machine that you will ever hold in your hands.

Bibliography

IT IS hard to think of a topic that rests on a wider base than does the study of landscapes. Virtually any shelf in any library can provide material which has some bearing on the subject. And yet the number of books and articles devoted specifically to landscapes is remarkably small. The study of landscapes is generally classified with more conventional subject areas, which can make the pursuit of relevant literature an interesting if sometimes frustrating and even overwhelming experience.

Outside of the efforts of landscape painters, the study of landscapes in their own right is a relatively new phenomena. A heightened awareness of landscapes has been fostered by the widespread awakening of environmental concerns and the popularization of ecological perspectives. The reader will notice that the preponderance of books about landscape date from the last decade or two. In Europe, and in Great Britain particularly, the study of landscapes seems to have gained legitimacy and acceptance more readily than in North America. The work of W. G. Hoskins is especially noteworthy, and makes exceptionally good reading because the author's passion for his subject exudes from every page. On this continent, J. B. Jackson stands out as the great pioneer of modern landscape studies. From 1951 until his retirement in 1968, he edited and wrote with keen insight for *Landscape*, a magazine which he founded. The best of his writings are collected in Zube, ed. *Landscapes*.

Perhaps the most generally useful book is Meinig, ed. *The Interpretation of Ordinary Landscapes*, especially the article by Peirce F. Lewis: "Axioms for Reading the Landscape: Some Guides to the American Scene." Forman and Godron *Landscape Ecology* and Watts *Reading the Landscape of America* both take an ecological point of view, but while the former is a text book which may be destined to become a classic, the latter is a sickly-sweet anecdotal journal which is, nevertheless, well worth browsing through. A fascinating theme is elaborately developed along literary lines in Marx *The Machine in the Garden*. Taking a philosophical approach, Relph *Place and Placelessness* and *Rational Landscapes and Humanistic Geography* offers many profound and original insights into commonplace landscapes, citing examples primarily in the Toronto area. The books also raise some discomforting moral questions—they should be required reading for all students of landscape architecture and related fields.

Chapman and Putnam *The Physiography of Southern Ontario* is the only book in its domain—it is indispensable. Clark *The Developing Canadian Community* is an outstanding sociological work. These fields are ably brought together in Harris and Warkentin *Canada Before Confederation*. Other useful contributions to the study of Ontario's historical geography can be found in Wood, ed. *Perspectives on Landscape and Settlement in Nineteenth Century Ontario*, and Spelt *Urban Development in South-Central Ontario*. The journal *Ontario History* occasionally features articles about landscape evolution: Kelly "Damaged and Efficient Landscapes in Rural and Southern Ontario 1870-1900," and McIlwraith "Altered Buildings: Another Way of Looking at the Ontario Landscape," are the best to date. *Ontario Geography*, an unrelated journal, can also be quite useful.

There are countless books about urban planning, development, and architecture, but the vast majority are dreadfully dull and undistinguished. Any of the works by Lewis Mumford rise above this sea of mediocrity, but they are weighty and fast becoming dated. The somewhat controversial ideas of Jane Jacobs and William Whyte are stimulating and worthy of contemplation. In the area of modern architecture, the journalistic genius of Tom Wolfe *From Bauhaus to Our House* is worth more than an entire shelf of books on the subject.

Finally, I am aware of two books that are based on the rephotography concept: the interesting volume by Koegler *Canada's Modern Landscape: An Air Photo Study*, and the lavishly reproduced Klett, et. al. *Second View: The Rephotographic Survey Project* which offers 130 pairs of meticulously matched photographs of the western American landscape. The rephotography process is explored in depth, but unfortunately there are no supporting captions explaining the changes in the individual landscapes.

Facing page: Morning mist on the Conestoga River, Waterloo R.M.

Appleton, Jay H. *The Experience of Landscape.* London: Wily, 1975.

Balch, R. E. *The Ecological Viewpoint: Five Radio Lectures as Heard on CBC University of the Air.* Toronto: CBC, 1965.

Battier, James Garnet. "Land Use History and Landscape Change Point Pelee National Park Ontario." Master's thesis, University of Western Ontario, 1975.

Bridgland, M. P. *Photographic Surveying.* Bulletin No. 56. Ottawa: Department of the Interior, 1924.

Brown, Ron. *Ghost Towns of Ontario.* Langley: Stagecoach, 1978.

Chapman, L. J., and D. F. Putnam. *The Physiography of Southern Ontario.* Toronto: Ontario Research Foundation, 1951; 3rd ed. Toronto: Ministry of Natural Resources, 1984.

Clark, Kenneth. *Landscape into Art.* London, John Murray, 1949; rpt. Boston: Beacon Press, 1961.

Clark, S. D. *The Developing Canadian Community.* Toronto: University of Toronto Press, 1962; rpt. 1968.

----------. *The Suburban Community.* Toronto: University of Toronto Press, 1964.

Cronon, William. *Changes in the Land: Indians, Colonists and the Ecology of New England.* New York: Hill and Wang; Toronto: McGraw-Hill Ryerson, 1983.

Dearden, Philip. *Landscape Aesthetics, An Annotated Bibliography.* Vol. no. 1220 of Council of Planning Librarians Exchange Bibliographies. Chicago: CPL Bibliographies, 1977.

Denhez, Marc. *Heritage Fights Back.* Ottawa: Heritage Canada; Toronto: Fitzhenry and Whiteside, 1978.

Eckbo, Garrett. *The Landscape We See.* New York: McGraw Hill, 1969.

Forman, Richard T. T., and Michel Godron. *Landscape Ecology.* New York: Wiley, 1986.

Frye, Northrop. *The Bush Garden: Essays on the Canadian Imagination.* Toronto: Anansi, 1971.

Glazebrook, G. P. deT. *A History of Transportation in Canada.* 2 Vol. Toronto: Ryerson, 1938; rpt. Toronto: McClelland and Stewart, 1964.

Gowans, Alan. *Building Canada: An Architectural History of Canadian Life.* Toronto: Oxford University Press, 1964.

Greenhill, Ralph and Verschoyle Beuson Blake. *Rural Ontario.* Toronto: University of Toronto Press, 1969.

Greenhill, Ralph, et. al. *Ontario Towns.* Ottawa: Oberon, 1974.

Greenhill, Ralph. *Early Photography in Canada.* Toronto: Oxford University Press, 1965.

Gross, Michael S., ed. *The Frontier Thesis and the Canadas: the Debate on the Impact of the Canadian Environment.* Toronto: Copp Clark, 1970.

Harris, R. Cole, and John Warkentin. *Canada Before Confederation: A Study in Historical Geography.* Toronto: Oxford University Press, 1974.

Hoskins, W. G. *The Making of the English Landscape.* (1955) Harmondsworth, Middlesex: Penguin, 1970.

Howison, John. *Sketches of Upper Canada: Domestic, Local and Characteristic.* Edinburgh: Oliver & Boyd, 1821; rpt. [New York]: Johnson Reprint, 1965; Toronto: Coles, 1970.

Jacobs, Jane. *Cities and the Wealth of Nations: Principles of Economic Life.* New York: Random House, 1984.

Jameson, Anna. *Winter Studies and Summer Rambles in Canada.* (1838) Toronto: McClelland and Stewart, 1923, 1965.

Jones, Robert Leslie. *History of Agriculture in Ontario 1613-1880.* Toronto: University of Toronto Press, 1946.

Kelly, Kenneth. "Damaged and Efficient Landscapes in Rural and Southern Ontario 1870-1900." *Ontario History* 66, no.1 (March 1974):1-14.

Kerr, Donald and Jacob Spelt. *The Changing Face of Toronto.* (Memoir II, Geographical Branch, Mines and Technical Surveys.) Ottawa: Queen's Printer, 1965.

Klett, Mark, et. al. *Second View: The Rephotographic Survey Project.* Albuquerque: University of New Mexico Press, 1984.

Koltun, Lilly. *City Blocks, City Spaces: Historical Photographs of Canada's Urban Growth c. 1850-1900.* Ottawa: P. A. A. Supplies and Services, 1980.

Koegler, John. *Canada's Modern Landscape: An Air Photo Study.* Toronto: Fisher, 1978.

Langman, R. C. *Patterns of Settlement in Southern Ontario: Three Studies.* Toronto: McClelland and Stewart, 1971.

Leighly, John, ed. *Land and Life: A Selection from the Writings of Carl Ortwin Sauer.* Berkeley: University of California Press, 1963.

Lemon, James T. *The Best Poor Man's Country: A Geographical Study of Early Southeastern Pennsylvania.* New York: Norton; Toronto: McLeod, 1976.

Marsh, George Perkins. *Man and Nature; or Physical Geography as Modified by Human Action.* New York: Scribner, 1864; rpt. Cambridge: Harvard University Press, 1965.

Marx, Leo. *The Machine in the Garden: Technology and the Pastoral Ideal in America.* New York: Oxford University Press, 1964.

McIlwraith, Thomas F. "Altered Buildings: Another Way of Looking at the Ontario Landscape." *Ontario History* 75, no.2 (June 1983): 111-134.

Meinig, D. W., ed. *The Interpretation of Ordinary Landscapes: Geographical Essays.* New York: Oxford University Press, 1979.

Mika, Helma and Nick Mika. *Places in Ontario: Their Name, Origins and History.* Encyclopedia of Ontario, Vol. 2. Belleville: Mika, 1977.

Morison, Samuel Eliot. *Samuel de Champlain: Father of New France.* Toronto: Little, Brown, 1972.

Mumford, Lewis. *The Highway and the City.* 1953; rpt. New York: Mentor, 1964.

Nelson, Howard J. "The Spread of an Artificial Landscape over Southern California." *Annals* 49, no.3 (1959): 80-100.

Nelson, J. G. *Man's Impact on the Western Canadian Landscape.* Toronto: McClelland and Stewart, 1976.

Plowden, David. *The Hand of Man on America.* Washington, DC: Smithsonian Institution Press, 1971.

Preston, Richard E. "The Recent Evolution of Ontario Central Place Systems in Light of Christaller's Concept of Centrality." *Canadian Geographical Journal* 23 (1979): 201-221.

Reeds, Lloyd G. "Agricultural Regions of Southern Ontario 1880 and 1951." *Economic Geography*, 35, (1959), 219-227. Reprinted with a supplement in Gentilcore, R. Louis ed. *Canada's Changing Geography*, Toronto: Prentice-Hall, 1967.

Relph, Edward C. *Place and Placelessness.* London: Pion, 1976.

----------. *Rational Landscapes and Humanistic Geography.* London: Croom Helm, 1981; and Totowa, NJ: Barnes and Noble, 1981.

Rempel, John. *Building With Wood and Other Aspects of Nineteen-Century Building in Ontario.* Toronto: University of Toronto Press, 1977.

Richardson, Douglas, ed. *Architecture in Ontario: A Selected Bibliography on Architectural Conservation and the History of Architecture.* Toronto: Ministry of Culture and Recreation, 1976.

Sadler, Barry and Allen Carlson, eds. *Environmental Aesthetics: Essays in Interpretation.* Western Geographical Series, no. 20. Victoria: University of Victoria Press, 1982.

Sloane, Eric. *Our Vanishing Landscape.* Funk & Wagnall,1955; rpt. New York: Ballantine; Toronto: Random House, 1974.

Smith, W. H. *Canada Past Present and Future.* Toronto: McClear, 1851; rpt. Belleville: Mika, 1973-1974.

Sontag, Susan. *On Photography.* New York: Farrar, Straus and Giroux, 1973.

Spelt, Jacob. *Urban Development in South-Central Ontario.* 1955; rpt. Toronto: McClelland and Stewart, 1972.

Stelter, G. A., and Alan F. J. Artibise. *Shaping the Urban Landscape: Aspects of the Canadian City Building Process.* Carleton Library Series. Ottawa: University of Ottawa Press, 1982.

Stilgoe, John R. *Common Landscapes of America: 1580-1845.* New Haven: Yale University Press, 1982.

Symons, Harry, and C.W. Jefferys. *Fences.* Toronto: McGraw-Hill Ryerson, 1958.

Tippett, Maria, and Douglas Cole. *From Desolation to Splendour: Changing Perceptions of the B. C. Landscape.* Vancouver: Clarke Irwin, 1977.

Walker, Gerald. "Farmers in the Urban Shadow: The Neighbourhood Effect and Neighbourhoods." *Ontario Geography* 22 (1983): 29-44.

Waterson, Elizabeth, and Douglas Hoffman, eds. *On Middle Ground: Landscape and Life in Wellington County 1841-1891.* Guelph: University of Guelph, 1974.

Watts, May Theilgaard. *Reading the Landscape of America.* New York: Collier-Macmillan, 1957; rpt. 1975.

Whebell, C. F. J., "Two Polygonal Settlement Schemes from Upper Canada." *Ontario Geography* 12 (1978): 85-92.

Whyte, William H. *The Last Landscape.* New York: Doubleday, 1968; rpt. 1970.

Wolfe, Tom. "From Bauhaus to Our House." *Harper's* 262-263 (June-July 1981): 33-54, 40-59. Also in book form. New York: Farrar, Straus and Giroux, 1981.

Wood, J. David, ed. *Perspectives on Landscape and Settlement in Nineteenth Century Ontario.* Toronto: McClelland and Stewart, 1975.

Wright, J. V. *Ontario Prehistory: An Eleven Thousand Year Outline.* Ottawa: National Museum of Man, 1972.

Zube, E. H., and M. J. Zube, ed. *Changing Rural Landscapes.* Amherst: University of Massachusetts, 1969.

Zube, Ervin H., ed. *Landscapes: Selected Writings of J. B. Jackson.* Amherst: University of Massachusetts, 1970.

Zube, Ervin H., Robert O. Brush, Julius Gy. Fabos, eds. *Landscape Assessment: Values, Perceptions, and Resourses.* Stroudsberg, Pa: Dowden, Hutchison and Ross, 1975.

Index of Place-names

Facing page: Sunset near Winterbourne, Waterloo R.M. Aug. 11, 1986.